Disney

Recent Titles in
Corporations That Changed the World

Toyota
K. Dennis Chambers

Harley-Davidson Motor Company
Missy Scott

Google
Virginia Scott

Apple, Inc.
Jason D. O'Grady

Starbucks
Marie Bussing-Burks

Southwest Airlines
Chris Lauer

Uber
B. Yasanthi Perera and Pia A. Albinsson

Starbucks, Second Edition
Marie A. Bussing

Disney

Stacy Mintzer Herlihy

Corporations That Changed the World

BLOOMSBURY ACADEMIC
NEW YORK • LONDON • OXFORD • NEW DELHI • SYDNEY

BLOOMSBURY ACADEMIC
Bloomsbury Publishing Inc
1385 Broadway, New York, NY 10018, USA
50 Bedford Square, London, WC1B 3DP, UK
29 Earlsfort Terrace, Dublin 2, Ireland

BLOOMSBURY, BLOOMSBURY ACADEMIC and the Diana logo are trademarks of Bloomsbury Publishing Plc

First published in the United States of America by ABC-CLIO 2022
Paperback edition published by Bloomsbury Academic 2025

Copyright © Bloomsbury Publishing Inc, 2025

For legal purposes the Acknowledgments on p. ix constitute an extension of this copyright page.

Cover photo: Walt Disney and Mickey Mouse statue at Disneyland.
(D. Hurst/Alamy Stock Photo)

All rights reserved. No part of this publication may be reproduced or transmitted in any form or by any means, electronic or mechanical, including photocopying, recording, or any information storage or retrieval system, without prior permission in writing from the publishers.

Bloomsbury Publishing Inc does not have any control over, or responsibility for, any third-party websites referred to or in this book. All internet addresses given in this book were correct at the time of going to press. The author and publisher regret any inconvenience caused if addresses have changed or sites have ceased to exist, but can accept no responsibility for any such changes.

Library of Congress Cataloging-in-Publication Data

Names: Herlihy, Stacy Mintzer, 1970- author.
Title: Disney / Stacy Mintzer Herlihy.
Description: Santa Barbara, California : Greenwood, an imprint of ABC-CLIO, LLC, [2022] | Series: Corporations that changed the world | Includes bibliographical references and index.
Identifiers: LCCN 2021030475 (print) | LCCN 2021030476 (ebook) | ISBN 9781440876011 (cloth) | ISBN 9781440876028 (ebook)
Subjects: LCSH: Disney, Walt, 1901-1966. | Walt Disney Company—History. | Motion picture studios—United States—History. | Corporations— United States—History. | Motion picture producers and directors—United States—Biography. | Executives—United States—Biography. | Animated films—United States—History and criticism. | Amusement parks—United States—History. | Disneyland (Calif.) | Walt Disney World (Fla.)
Classification: LCC PN1999.W27 H47 2022 (print) | LCC PN1999.W27 (ebook) | DDC 791.43092—dc23
LC record available at https://lccn.loc.gov/2021030475
LC ebook record available at https://lccn.loc.gov/2021030476

ISBN: HB: 978-1-4408-7601-1
PB: 979-8-7651-3897-7
ePDF: 978-1-4408-7602-8
eBook: 979-8-2160-7517-2

Series: Corporations That Changed the World

To find out more about our authors and books visit www.bloomsbury.com and sign up for our newsletters.

*For Brendan Thomas Herlihy Jr., Serena Jane Herlihy,
and Charlotte Winifred Herlihy*

Contents

Acknowledgments		ix
Introduction		xi
Chapter 1	The Main Street That Never Was: The Life and Legacy of Walt Disney	1
Chapter 2	From Steamboat Willie to Buzz Lightyear: Disney and the Establishment of the American Animation Industry	25
Chapter 3	Disneyland, Disney World, and the Creation of Southern California and Florida in the Public Mind	45
Chapter 4	The Hat That Began It All: Spinoffs and Merchandise for Every Occasion	71
Chapter 5	Princesses, Politics, and a Different Audience: Controversies That Continue to Challenge Perceptions Today	89
Chapter 6	An Empire of Imagination: New Directions for Disney	113
Bibliography		135
Index		139

Acknowledgments

I would like to thank the following people for their help: Brendan Thomas Herlihy Jr., Serena Jane Herlihy, Charlotte Winifred Herlihy, Tish Davidson, Allison Hagood, Alice Wasney, Aubrey Collins, Marsha Disbrow, Anna U. Mormack, Judy Mollen Walters, Mike P. Guerriero, Cigal Shaham, Jody Mullen, Renee Lisa, Ursyl Kukura-Straw, Diana Austin, Miriam Safira Simon Zarovsky, Janette Zdunczyk Ratliff, Trice Badesso, and Catherine Lafuente.

I would like to extend my sincerest thanks to Pamela Brown Margolis. Her insights were extremely useful in helping me craft an important section of this book.

I would also like to thank my editor, Maxine Taylor, for her help in creating this book. This is a better manuscript thanks to her thoughtful, informed suggestions.

Introduction

Watching a Disney movie or visiting a Disney park is one of the most American of all rites of passage. Disney is where Americans and the rest of the world go to find a classic experience that defines what it means to be an American. The hot sun, familiar rides, and mouse ears tell us where we are and what we're going to do. We've all been here before. Walt Disney and his world are intrinsically part of the United States, and forever ours from our toddler years onward. American childhoods are spent watching Disney movies. Family vacations mean a Disney park in the hot Florida or California sun. Grown-ups return to parks with their kids to create (or re-create) happy family memories. As adults, we all love knowing there's a bit more to the mouse and the ears. All Americans are part of Disney's world in some way.

Disney is one of a handful of historical names that are intimately tied to the creation and history of the modern United States of America. Like Ben Franklin, George Washington, Abraham Lincoln, Amelia Earhart, Neil Armstrong, and Barack Obama, Walt Disney comes to mind when thinking of the very notion of what it means to be part of the United States. Disney is as American as warmed-over apple pie and melted Velveeta. The Disney name immediately conjures up an America that is carefree, warm, wholesome, and happy. This is the original, supposedly true and authentic United States as people see it even today. Disney's America is where rural farming and small business ownership meet and combine in an overlay of ever-expanding industrial progress. Beneath the apparently smooth surface lies a fascinating, complicated, and worthwhile story. The placid exterior of this world, like the man behind it, concealed a far more complex and much more interesting interior.

Disney began his life in Chicago, spent his childhood in small-town Missouri, and rose to fame in Hollywood. The seemingly unpretentious man with the shelf full of Oscars was America's modest, folksy Uncle Walt. He rose to fame in part because of his uncanny ability to be in tune with the lives and wishes of so many Americans. His successors would bring the company even more fame and turn his modest studio into an entertainment juggernaut.

Underneath the sunny exterior of Disney's life, career, and the company that has been at the heart of American life for decades, there lie contradictions that offer insights into the fissures that tell us much about American life as Americans have lived it. Disney's career plans started as a simple series of drawings that he hoped would sell well, earn money, and allow him to become a newspaper cartoonist. Animation was his creative outlet, one that let him escape the grim reality of his teenage years. Almost offhand doodles that others further refined are now a historic part of the American landscape that remains as vividly imprinted on the world as ever. His ideas about the perfect all-American vacation came to characterize the American concept of fun with family and transformed Florida and California into the places they remain today.

Disney's willingness to embrace technology even when it was unclear if it would pay off financially made him a pioneer of great insight during his own lifetime and beyond. He and his team of animators pushed concepts that found applications in many other fields, from movies to personal computing and the act of buying entertainment-related products. His profound love of music and determination to create an entire experience for the viewer once the curtain came up brought his medium to new heights, even as it nearly ruined his first full-scale animation production financially.

At his death in 1966, he was at the zenith of his fame. He was as much of a beloved icon as Mickey, the mouse that would forever be part of his heritage. The world mourned even as people wildly celebrated what his sheer grit had brought into their own lives. Since that era, the company he left behind continues to play a role in many important global industries. Disney has also helped formulate policies on subjects ranging from artificial intelligence to the treatment of those with disabilities. His is a legacy that continues to play a starring role in how the world sees the United States, from large European cities to tiny Pacific island nations. Disney worlds, both in movies and across continents, are part of the allure of America for billions of people.

Disney grew with the century and his native land. From his birth in 1901 until his death six-and-a-half decades later, his was a world in which

Introduction

Americans were undeniably ascendant. His conception of the perfect America created the perception of the country for generations both at home and abroad. Disney's upbringing on a Missouri farm in small-town America lasted only a few scant years, but he doused these years in deep nostalgia, brought them to life for others, and turned his memories into a touchstone for American life.

In his later years, Walt Disney made further leaps into the notion of the ideal American place with the modernist world of Epcot and the sentimental urban planning of Celebration, Florida, which became reality after his death. His fundamentally unclouded vision obscured the hard times of his early childhood and the cruelty of his life as a teen.

His spotless America, where people can be deliciously, fully at ease while cradled in comfort, is there for the taking when people enter a Disney theme park. The second they walk in, guests see Walt Disney's personal vision of an idealized America in the form of Main Street U.S.A. They wait behind a park that is set artfully just out of sight of the larger world beyond it. Forced perspective means that buildings along Main Street are only seven-eighths the height of a standard building. Buildings get even smaller as people look up. This is the same perspective that he brought to his work. Things are not always what they appear. The man who created cartoons for children and gave kids an after-school Mickey Mouse Club offers a street seen from a child's perspective. Giving visitors the sense that an ideal childhood is there to enjoy again and again remains part of the appeal of his work and an essential aspect of his ultimate legacy.

The darker shadows behind the streets, costumes, shops, and cafés along this opening to another world offer no smell of dung or unwanted sights beyond the pastel colors. There's no hint of the widespread malnutrition that was the fate of so many young people when Walt Disney was a young man. They do not suggest the world of women and minorities without basic rights, toiling hard from dawn to well past dusk without comfortable homes or electricity. Even as so much of his work focused on children, the adult Walt left the realities of his own childhood behind. He rarely spoke of getting up early in the morning before school so he could service a paper route and help his family survive economically. The childhood he made for visitors has little in common with his own family's terrible struggles. The well-kept streets and smiling faces of Disney employees do not reference his many years of toil, either personally or professionally. They also do little to reflect the company's often-tempestuous relationship with the employees who make the entire experience possible. Walt kept to the shiny ideal, despite an early bankruptcy that hit him hard in his early twenties. His later animation efforts were aimed at bringing quality products to the public, even in the face of mountains of bills that might have daunted another man. Life for him would be a lot harder than the happy Disney facade ever implied.

The reality of war and competition from other media do not intrude either. With Disney's help, Mickey and Minnie Mouse have a place in the world of pop culture today, even as they no longer appear in Pixar cartoons for a swooning audience. Fans can buy mouse ears in a dozen rainbow colors at his parks and see the shorts where they first appeared in black and white before anyone even thought a full-length animation feature a realistic possibility. Movies like *Bambi* were once such flops with the public that they nearly sunk his studio, but they have earned back the enormous sums it took to bring them to life. Perhaps even more satisfying for him, many of his films have earned the status of American classics for historians and the public alike. This is what he and the company he started brought to the United States. Disney's America took moviegoers to places like Neverland and Tomorrowland, where the entire world could unfold at their feet with ease. Throughout Disney's lifetime and beyond, however, there were troubles just below the surface.

Disney gave big-screen life to some of the worst excesses of American racism and failed to provide credit to the women who drew everything from the dancing flowers of *Fantasia* to the backdrops for the It's a Small World After All ride. He refused to offer the hardworking people at his company a decent share of the profits. His world is the world of many Americas at the same time. Here, young girls of all backgrounds can finally be princesses and indulge in the fantasy of life with a happily ever after. But that same world offers little for the young girl who would rather put on pants, find adventures of her own, and discard her fairy wings when she reaches for her own adulthood.

For Americans today and for the rest of the world, Disney continues to be what it has been for decades. Nearly all American kids of all ethnic backgrounds watch Disney movies, dream of visiting Disneyland, and think about the world through the company's eyes during their childhood. Disney is still one of the first things that many people all over the world think of when they think of the United States. For better or worse, however deeply attractive, charming, and yet profoundly imperfect it may be, Disney was, is, and remains a central part of the American Dream, written on a global canvas of imagination.

CHAPTER ONE

The Main Street That Never Was: The Life and Legacy of Walt Disney

Behind the facade that Walt Disney brought to his work was a man who lived through incredibly turbulent times and wasn't always on the right side of history. As Disney experienced wars and economic turmoil, the country he understood on so many levels became a superpower and took its place as one of the world's most influential nations. Over the course of his 65 years, he saw almost constant national and world conflict. Two world wars and the start of an ongoing Cold War defined his life and how he saw the United States and the world beyond its shores. Against this canvas of uncertainty, he was almost entirely driven by a relentless, cheerful optimism that he and his company transmitted to the world. Disney and the characters he created offered joy and happiness to millions in times of profound sorrow. Walt Disney played a crucial hand in providing the world with a view of the United States that it could not resist. He would shape it in ways that he could not have imagined as a young man.

A Hardscrabble Childhood

Walt Disney designed a worldwide vision of childhood in his movies that is deeply beguiling. The idea of a jaunty, pleasant American childhood in which children are free to explore the world around them unfettered is crucial to Disney's worldview. He gave his fans the impression that he was drawing on his own life experiences for direct inspiration. He cultivated this idea to friends and the American public, but he left out many details that he did not care to reveal unless people looked very closely. As he grew into "Uncle Walt," his early years formed many bands of important memories that he used as his inspiration. A kernel of hard, raw truth was buried in layers of shiny coating that left little room for real life. Disney's own childhood began on a different note. Like so many others of his generation, his own youth was short, and then over quite quickly. For a man who later defined the essential notion of a wonderful childhood for millions, his formative years were largely about hard work, and often profoundly bitter disappointment.

Walter Elias Disney entered the world on December 5, 1901. While his family would sometimes imply that they were descended from the aristocratic d'Isigny family of Normandy, Walter made his own appearance in the bustling, all-American city of Chicago. His family came here by a circuitous route that began in England and then passed through Ireland. From there, his grandfather settled in Canada. Tired of farming and the cruel winters they had not expected, his grandfather and father made their way south, all the way to Florida, years before Walt was born. Despite his own son's later shaping the very concept of the state of Florida, Elias Disney found the weather warmly inviting, but the way of life itself hard going. After his first orange crop failed, he could not make a living. Elias Disney and his wife, Flora Call, decided it was time to head north to Chicago. The Chicago of their day was a place poised for tremendous expansion, and they wanted to be part of it. The city on the banks of Lake Michigan was in the very heart of the Midwest. Golden-haired Walt, the youngest of four brothers and two years older than his sister Ruth, lived here until he was four. His father made a living building houses for people with the same goals in life. Frustrated by the city's occasionally louche alleyways and clinging to an ideal of personal independence, his deeply religious parents decided that it was time for a change of scenery yet again. This choice lingered in Walt's memory long after and set the tone for memories that he would make an integral part of the United States many decades later. His father sold his city home and went off to farm on the outskirts of Marceline, Missouri.

Today, rural Marceline is home to roughly 2,300 people. That's about half the population it had when the Disney family showed up, ready to try their hand at tilling the land again. Marceline is an archetypal American small town about a two-hour drive from Kansas City, Missouri. At that time, it was one of the many railroad towns connecting larger municipalities like Chicago and St. Louis like pearls on a necklace. Walt and his siblings found a children's paradise waiting for them everywhere they went. The 45 acres that his father bought at the edge of the community offered orchards teeming with fresh fruit and a dozen other inviting spaces. Many types of wild game crossed the fields each season. Half a dozen different kinds of farm animals were ready for them to watch, including the pigs that he gave names before they were eaten.

Walt and his sister entered school at nearly the same time. School held far less appeal than the open fields for dreamy Walt, who began to spend his spare time drawing. He and his siblings spent their free time roaming the fields their father had purchased. They went swimming in the summer, caught fish for supper, skated on the frozen town ponds each winter, and participated in all the joyful rituals of small-town life. From the Fourth of July to the Christmas holidays, this was one of the few (if not only) periods in his life when he could do almost anything he wanted with his time.

It was not to last. In 1910, his father, stubbornly refusing to use fertilizer, failed at farming again. Elias Disney sold the farm. He rented a home for a brief time so his youngest son and daughter could finish the school year, and then moved the family to Kansas City the following year. Just as Marceline would come to define Walt, so would the rougher streets of humming Kansas City shape the course of his outlook in life, even as he attempted to ignore this part of his passage into manhood. The city that his parents found was a large place for the Midwest, with over 150,000 residents. A grid of parks and boulevards defined the community and offered many places to stroll on a weekend or after work. One of the nation's largest networks of electrified streetcars crisscrossed the city's streets and made for easy and thrilling trips from one neighborhood to the next.

Disney's father continued to struggle financially. His inability to make a decent living as an adult would have an impact on Walt Disney's teen years. His father would essentially ruin his youngest son's childhood with his demands that Walt give up much of his time to support the family. Elias Disney ultimately chose to enlist the help of his two youngest sons to put food on the table and a roof over their heads. The head of the family purchased a Kansas City paper route that served over 600 customers. His was a large route that required a lot of incredibly hard work just to meet customers' expectations of brand-new newspapers twice a day on their front porches. The route required him and his family to keep to the same area of the city at all times. This was the only way to manage the physical demands necessary to provide service to several hundred people. At the tender age of nine, Walt Disney was ordered by his father to get up at 3:30 a.m. every day of the week, even on Sundays. His unrelenting routine working for his father meant that he not only had to get up early, but he had to leave school half an hour early to deliver the afternoon paper to expectant customers. The youngest Disney son was allowed almost no free time of his own. Unlike many of his peers, he was not given the chance to have a close-up look at the many wonderful experiences of Kansas City in the same way that he had done in Marceline. Worst of all, his father took nearly all the money his sons earned, despite promises to the contrary. For the next six years, Walt Disney devoted most of his time, hours each day, to handing out papers. For him, life as a teen was all about getting up as early as possible, rushing to snatch a quick breakfast, sitting in school for a few hours, and then heading off again to repeat the same process of paper delivery. Disney would credit the paper route with instilling in him a sense of how to manage his time. He would also tell people that it created the discipline that would come to characterize his life in the public eye. At the same time, he confessed to being haunted by the trauma of the route and how it robbed him of his ability to do everything from engaging in after-school sports to getting a good night's sleep. What saved him in the end were his own innate qualities of determination, ambition, and a willful, deliberate idealism that he let fall on this part of his life like a curtain at the end of a play.

By the time Walt was sixteen, he was ready to leave the world of formal education and his father's demands behind forever. World War I was in progress, and he wanted to be part of the action. His father sold off the paper route. That freed his son from the bleak grind. Technically still too young to enter the war, Walt and a friend enlisted in the Red Cross Ambulance Corps, as they were less picky about age than the U.S. military. Forging his official age on the permission slip from his parents, he left high school without a diploma and went off to train in Chicago, and then to France. The months he spent driving a truck and helping out soldiers marked his transition from childhood to becoming a full-fledged adult, ready to strike out on his own. He would return to the United States a grownup, with $600 in savings in hand, determined to leave his family behind and find a place in the art world. Disney still spent his spare time drawing and imagining art as his eventual career.

In his teens, his father had allowed him to take a few classes at the Chicago Academy of Fine Arts. This brief training convinced him of two things. In the first place, he realized that he was not a fine artist. Instead, a single class in cartooning made him realize exactly where his talents lay. His challenge was to find a way to earn a living from what was a true passion in him. At first, he wanted to become a newspaper cartoonist. This ambition quickly evolved into something different. In his late teens, Walt Disney decided he wanted to join the ranks of the people who were calling themselves by a new title: *animators*. With that in mind, he studied everything he could get his hands on in this developing and rapidly expanding field. While working a full-time job as a commercial artist for the Kansas City Film Ad Company, he worked on his own animation technique. The great self-confidence that marked almost everything else he did in life led him to decide that it was time to become a businessman, create his own cartoons, form a studio, and even hire others.

Laugh-O-Gram Studio was actually his second effort at a studio of his own. He formed his first, Iwerks-Disney Commercial Artists, with a coworker and fellow artist, Ub Iwerks. The two set up a fast and offhand venture. Iwerks would go on to become a legend in the field. He played a major role in many areas of animation for Disney, such as creating a more likeable Mickey Mouse and starting a number of other animation studios. Their first effort was ultimately dissolved for lack of clients. The second studio went bankrupt in two years, but set the stage for the rest of Disney's early career and made animation history. He and his fellow animators cranked out a series of short films based on his personal interpretation of various kinds of fables. The studio failed for many reasons. Even this did not daunt Disney, however, who was convinced that he could conquer this medium and earn a living at the same time. At 21, he had just enough money for a train ticket to Los Angeles. Hollywood would prove to be a natural fit with his deep-seated tenacity and sheer self-confidence.

Making His Way West

When Walt Disney left Kansas City for LA, there were several other regions and cities that were becoming important for any animator hoping to make a career in the field. Disney could have made his way east to New York City to accomplish the same goals. New York was a major center of animation at that time, and very much at the forefront of technological innovation. But Disney decided that brash California, an up-and-comer in the still-forming world of animation, would give him a better chance at making his own mark. The warm weather and smaller town also seemed filled with more possibilities than the already-established New York City. He brought with him samples of his earlier work from the failed animation studio effort in Kansas City and a buoyant sense of belief in his own talents. This, remarkably, would prove to be enough to open doors in Los Angeles—and open them incredibly quickly. With the help of his brother Roy, who was recovering from tuberculosis but wanted to be part of the venture, they formed another studio. This one was centered around the production of yet more animated features. Disney Bros. soon had a contract with a distributor named Margaret Winkler to produce a series of early animated shorts for movie distribution.

In the mid-1920s, Los Angeles was a proving ground for Disney. The energy of the city allowed him to tap into the work of others in the local animation community who came to the community from far away for the same reasons. The studio also enabled him to hone his art and imagine where animation might lead. His early work, like so much of the animation of the day, was noteworthy for a few basic qualities. The emphasis at the time was on crude gags intended to get an easy laugh. Fast production to meet hard quotas for the awaiting movie audience was the norm. The goal, at least for Disney, was to take each of his works and learn how to make the next one better. His first Hollywood studio was ultimately taken over by Charles Mintz, Margaret Winkler's husband, in 1929. Mintz pulled the studio out from under Disney by hiring nearly all his employees away with a better contract. A disillusioned Disney decided that he would never work for anyone else again. He also decided to start all over again. While Mintz's underhanded tactics infuriated Walt Disney, it also led him to the birth of Mickey Mouse and the start of an American realm of his own.

This was the era of changes quickly taking the movie industry in new directions. One of the most important developments at the end of the 1920s was learning not only how to use sound in film, but also how to use it effectively. For Disney, sound was a natural fit with his work. Sound worked with his ideas about how to craft the perfect animated features. Sound paired with animation struck many of his colleagues as strange and unnatural. The first motion picture that made use of the spoken word and combined it with characters was *The Jazz Singer,* featuring Al Jolson.

People talked in that 1927 movie. The notion that a cartoon might do the same struck many in the industry as bizarre. Walt Disney's previous ventures had been all about silent animation. Audiences were expected to give voice to the action in their own heads. His new idea of marrying music and synchronized sound side effects to drawings on screen met resistance from more than one person at Disney Bros. This was in part because of the expense. His cartoons were not cheap, barely breaking even at best. The idea of putting another layer of money on top of everything else was frightening to his backers. Disney ignored the critics because he knew it not only could work, but also add something special to the end product. The first fully successful feature the studio made with this synchronized animation technique was *Steamboat Willie*. Released in 1928, it was slightly under six minutes long. The short film was an instant hit. Spectators loved the way that the sounds Disney animators used created a more coherent storyline. Critics responded with enthusiastic praise. What was once a series of moving drawings and little else was now a more realized and vivid form that entranced and delighted people of all ages.

Disney bet almost everything he had on this new concept. He borrowed against his home and even asked his frugal, stolid father for a loan. Just as before, financial issues presented a problem. His team of financial backers found cash flow a constant issue as the studio worked. Fiscal and creative challenges continued even more in the years ahead. Despite this reality, Disney savored the moment. *Steamboat Willie* was the public's first real introduction to the character of Mickey Mouse. Disney forged ahead, confident that he had created something entirely new. As it turns out, he had. Merging sound with a cartoon character at the same time pushed him and his studio far ahead of others in the animation business. Competitors simply could not keep up. They would largely concede the field to him in the coming years, only to reclaim it later when World War II intervened and the studio's vision began to stagnate.

Mickey Mouse changed everything in Disney's life and career. Working with Columbia Pictures for distribution purposes, and then later United Artists and RKO, he quickly made the character a hit not only in the United States, but internationally. Widespread dissemination made Mickey and his adventures much talked about and almost wholly admired overseas in many nations, including Germany, France, and the United Kingdom. With the release of the ninth Mickey Mouse animated feature in 1929, *The Karnival Kid,* Mickey Mouse spoke his first words. They were "Hot dog," and Disney was the one who said them. Walt Disney became the voice of Mickey Mouse in part because he wanted it done to his satisfaction. The decision to make his voice known to people all over the world extended his fame even further. Animated features were embraced by people from all walks of life, but the studio was not earning a lot of money. This was due in part to Disney's unwillingness to compromise on quality. To him, quality meant that every single detail had to be right before a work was considered ready for the public. That meant pursuing certain storylines and then discarding them later, even if this did not make sense financially. Money was, and always would be, merely fodder for him to create more and better animation. During the Great Depression, Disney encountered a frustrated and sad audience hungry for some measure of happiness, if only for a short while in a darkened room. With so little work available, he could hire excellent animators at bargain basement rates. People wanted to work at Disney. A job there was prestigious, creative, and often well-paying if the artist was a Disney favorite. Animators stayed even if it meant sometimes dealing with Disney the perfectionist, who might openly tear into their work and throw away days or even months of carefully drawn scenes.

After his first success, Disney had fame and a clear audience willing to follow where he led. This was especially true in the midst of the Great Depression, when pockets were empty and jobs scarce. He wanted something more. Not content with the animation process as it stood, even with sound, Disney drove his artists harder to get at the ingrained qualities of the characters they brought to life. For him, the objective when creating animated films was not merely a series of gags and a few laughs, as it was for many others at that time. He wanted to create characters and have the animation flow from the ideas the characters evoked in the public's mind. The quick success of Mickey Mouse made possible the next level of animation he had in mind: color and a full-length story.

The 1930s brought Walt Disney into the public eye and made him virtually public property. Everyone watched his short films, including presidents, ministers, and audiences desperate to escape the realities of difficult times. The shorts were deeply satisfying as a form of ongoing revenue and a means of branding for the studio. However, they were not advancing the art form in the way that Disney wanted it done. His initial Mickey Mouse films were followed by a series of shorts known as the *Silly Symphonies*. The *Silly Symphonies* brought the entire studio intense acclaim. Within 10 years, it had received many kudos, including the Academy Award for Best Animated Short Film seven times. Shorts were provided to movie-going audiences on a set schedule. Every two weeks, there was a new feature. For Disney Studios, this meant a team capable of producing about literally seventy-five feet of animation in a single day. Animation of this sort was a monumental undertaking that had not been done on this scale before, anywhere in the world.

Even while meeting this hugely demanding schedule, Disney believed that there was an audience for a much longer feature. He wanted one that told a well-known story audiences would know even before they saw his movie. He also wanted to avoid using one of his existing characters while bringing in music and color. After a careful search, he settled on *Snow White and the Seven Dwarfs*. Fables had inspired his first animation and became his inspiration again. Nearly 500 people were employed at the studio, a huge number on an unprecedented scale. They worked on all the projects he had going on by the time the project officially began in February 1936. Walt Disney was there every single step of the way. Everything from the names of the dwarves to the colors used during each scene was part of his overall concept. Nothing went into the movie without his personal approval. The painstaking process took up nearly all his waking hours. Not until December 1937 would *Snow White* come to the big screen. Disney was not entirely satisfied with the finished product, but the studio was running out of money. They needed the revenue from the movie to pay back their loans. This meant he had to leave imperfections in the final product. Prince Charming shimmied on screen, and Disney let him because he didn't have the necessary money to correct the mistake. He would release the film for the promised Christmas rush. These flaws would be corrected later when the film was rereleased in theaters for a second chance at earning money.

Flaws and all, the movie was a huge hit with the public and the critics. Critics gave it rave reviews, and audiences showed up in droves. Within a year and a half, the film was a financial hit. Earnings for his film in the United States alone were over $6.5 million. This was a tremendous sum for any movie at the time, let alone an animated feature. The enormous returns on their initial investment let Walt and Roy pay back their loans and start new projects. In one sense, releasing *Snow White* marked the end of an era that Walt had begun largely on his own. The film showed that it was possible to create a full-length, animated feature film and gain the public's attention, money, and critical acclaim.

For Walt and his animators, the film also led to questions about where to go with their new art form in the coming years. The time leading up to and just after World War II saw further refinement of his ideas. These new ideas led to movies that would eventually enter the canon of adored American childhood films. *Snow White* brought together speech, color, and music. His film also brought an opportunity to bring audiences to the theater for a film geared to children and adults at the same time. These concepts formed the basis of the features the studio brought to the public in the next few years. Most of his work in the next decades focused on the world of wholesome family entertainment. From feature films and efforts like the Mickey Mouse Club, Disney practically created the genre of the family film.

Three full-length pictures, *Pinocchio, Fantasia,* and *Dumbo* were the focus of the studio's prewar work. Each brought a different idea about animation to the public. *Pinocchio* was the immediate follow-up to *Snow White*. Like *Snow White*, it was intended to be a lighthearted story that parents and kids alike could enjoy. The original was a dark story by the Italian author Carlo Collodi, published several decades before Disney read it. Disney found the original main character unlikeable. In his hands, *Pinocchio* got less naughty and much nicer. He also got a sidekick, in the form of Jiminy Cricket as his moral conscience. Despite the fact that

Disney made the main character sweeter, the film stuck to a grittiness that Disney wanted when it came to the depiction of the physical world. It had an intense realism at every stage that fit well with the process of creating a fully believable wood puppet who becomes a little boy. Realistic effects such as the transformation of weather into rain on screen made this film another artistic triumph for the studios.

In Disney's eyes, animation could serve to mirror the best of the natural world and immortalize it on film. Animation for him was a showcase that could bring to life realistic yet beautiful art. Released in 1940, the feature went on to win two Academy Awards: Best Original Song and Best Music: Original Score. This was the first time an animated feature won an Academy Award in a nonanimated category. Despite its critical success, the film was not a hit at the box office. Unlike *Snow White*, *Pinocchio* could not be distributed overseas due to World War II. Early battles cut off a major source of profits. The second feature would eventually earn far more than the $2 million it cost to make, but when released, it was a serious financial disappointment that left the studio mired in debt.

Dumbo was another effort that would enter the canon of great American animated movies. The film was intended as a fast piece of animation to earn the studio as much money as possible, as quickly as possible. Artistry was part of the process, but only so long as it fit in with the studio's financial needs. The goal was to be fast and grab the public's attention. At just over an hour, it's also one of the shortest long-form Disney features of this period. Created with a relatively small budget of roughly $1 million, *Dumbo* earned a profit of nearly double that when it was released in 1941, right before the attack on Pearl Harbor. Audiences liked the simple storyline and easy-to-understand animation as much as critics did. *Dumbo* may have been the most financially successful movie of the prewar era. However, it was a different movie that garnered the lion's share of Disney's attention right before the U.S. entry into World War II.

Fantasia was, in many ways, Disney's most personal film. Walt Disney's formal education was no more than a single year of high school, and included little musical training. Even without a formal background in the art, Walt was confident that he could bring classical music to life and do for classical music what he had done for cartooning. Spanning eight separate sections set to orchestral music, the film is about Disney's belief that animation could be as much higher art as a series of gags or a simple fairy tale for children. *Fantasia* was a collaboration between Disney, hundreds of animators, and world-renowned conductor Leopold Stokowski. With characteristic enthusiasm and the sort of hubris that had brought him to

Los Angeles in the first place, Disney believed that the film was going to be an aesthetic milestone that would continue to transform the animation world. Animators at his studio were not entirely convinced this was the right direction to go in after straightforward, character-driven movies like *Snow White*. Many felt that *Fantasia* was pretentious and leaden. Released in 1940, the film was greeted with great critical acclaim from the first few reviewers. Unfortunately, it was largely downhill afterward. Later reviews were mixed. Using a new technology known as Fantasound that aimed at richer harmonics offered thrills that enhanced the feel of watching the film. The system may have been Walt's darling, but it was costly to install and limited the picture's release potential. In later years, Disney officials made many changes to the original, including editing it down and reissuing it multiple times. Disney's goal had been to bring out a new version of *Fantasia* every few years. An entirely new film wasn't released until 1999, under the direction of Walt's nephew. *Fantasia* would also be greeted with far better reviews in later years. Critics hailed it as a hugely significant piece of American animation, even as they reexamined certain flaws, such as racist and sexist imagery.

During the War

World War II began in Europe in 1939. While the war would not touch American shores for a few years, the early days of the war had a big impact on the function of Disney Studios. The war cut off film distribution channels and major sources of revenue that had helped pay the enormous costs of making animation. With such avenues shut off, the studio was not doing well financially. For much of the war years, *Bambi* was the primary focus of the studio. Animators worked on the film for over five years, from first conception in 1937 until it was finally released to the public in 1942. Many critics were not happy with the move almost entirely away from human characters. Audiences disliked the film's darker elements and felt that it was too intense for small children. Like so many other films, this Disney feature achieved great critical and financial success many years after it was released. At that time, however, it was a financial disaster, with a loss of over $200,000. Studio officials were left struggling fiscally yet again and looking for more projects anywhere they could find them. Disney and his staffers found their salvation in government-subsidized films that, while not particularly creative or memorable, allowed the studio to wait out the war's resolution and pay off some of their creditors. These films also provided some of the studio's arguably most enduring and practical work. Work during this period filled diverse objectives; subjects ranged from pushing American support for the war, mocking Hitler, and shoring up mosquito eradication efforts in the Caribbean.

Even before American entry into the war, Disney saw possibilities in working directly with the government. His contacts in government opened doors and brought in minor business from government officials happy to have Disney on their side. In the aftermath of the bombing of Pearl Harbor, he began his government work with a film urging Americans to pay taxes to help fund the war effort. Ironically, it was not a fiscal success. He and his employees spent the rest of the war essentially engaging in two ventures. The first was a series of animated shorts aimed at the open South American market. The second were varied types of direct propaganda films, intended to advance the Allied cause, encourage men to enlist in the armed forces, and remind people back home to support the war. Disney undertook this step with great reluctance. Surrendering creativity to government officials made him deeply unhappy, even as he supported the overall plan to oust Nazism from Europe.

Government officials were concerned about the rise of fascism in Europe and the possibility that this ideology would spread even farther, to Latin America. American officials saw the world-famous Walt Disney as the perfect ambassador to open hearts and minds south of the border to the Allied cause. President Roosevelt sent Disney and more than a dozen staffers on a tour of three South American nations in 1941. Under the auspices of a government post known as the Coordinator of Inter-American Affairs (CIAA), Disney and a small band of high-level staffers met with prominent Latin American leaders. They also studied regional culture and looked for ways to incorporate the existing artistic culture into Disney's animation efforts. The two-month tour led to two major films and the production of many animation shorts.

Saludos Amigos was the first effort that came from the tour. Composed of four shorts and live-action footage of major Latin American cities, it is an odd piece. Running at a mere 42 minutes, the film was released in 1943. The *New York Times* called the movie "gentle satire laced in with jovial fun." Some critics credit the film with giving residents of the United States a taste of different aspects of Latino culture that had not been seen before in the country in any meaningful way. Disney followed up with another feature-length film, *The Three Caballeros*. This was the first Disney movie to combine live action sequences with animation. A vaguely more mature Donald Duck lusts after actual women. When combined with a certain level of surreal imagery that did not appear to make initial sense, it baffled critics and audiences alike. Some critics later argue that Disney merely served as a propaganda arm of the ruling class in the United States and dictators in the region at this time with such films, rather than as a catalyst for change. *Jacobin Magazine* says of their efforts, "Today, it seems clear that the two Disney pictures established a precedent in which the film industry would work to justify American intervention in the region and around the globe." Both films were moderate hits with the public both north and south of the border.

The second part of the work of Disney Studios work during World War II was wholly devoted to all aspects of the ongoing war, both at home and abroad. Animators and live-action experts turned out yards of different types of war films intended for educational and propaganda purposes. The stats were startling. Over 400,000 feet of film were brought to screen as the war continued. Disney films explained everything from new war laws to the army enlistment process. They were offered at cost, enabling the studio to stay afloat without making a profit or paying down its overall debt. The studio was actually millions of dollars in debt as late as 1944. Films were not the only thing that Disney officials did to help the Allies. There were war posters with Disney characters, along with books about the long-term aims of the Allies. There were also armed forces patches featuring Disney art. A five-person unit worked on site, creating individual patches for over 1,300 army units. War bonds even featured characters from *Snow White*. U.S. Treasury Department officials credited Disney Studios with selling more than $50 million to finance the war to investors both large and small.

Walt Disney remained determinedly apolitical during the course of his early career. He said little during the Great Depression but made it clear in subtle ways that he leaned left, as his parents had. He and many of his employees saw the war as a chance to increase the association of the studio with uncomplicated American patriotism. Many cartoons produced during this time were jingoistic, with elementary themes of good and evil. The 1943 animated feature *Der Führer's Face* made fun of the Nazis head on and linked the fight against Nazism directly with Disney's characters in the public mind. Of all the work the studio did at this time, one film was his particular favorite. Walt Disney was the driving force behind a production called *Victory through Air Power*. Based on the work of Alexander P. de Seversky, it argues in favor of aviation as the key to war victory. This was his most personal film during the war period, and one that he hoped would be taken seriously by the Allied leaders. The film was also one of the studio's most lasting contributions to American history. President Roosevelt saw it and decided that American war interests were best served by the long-range bombing process via the use of aircraft. Many shorts produced during this time had an immediate effect on people's lives. Films like *The Winged Scourge*, the first of many Disney health-related films during the war years, aimed at better relations between the Americas. Here, the dwarves of *Snow White* showed residents of nations such as Cuba how to get rid of mosquitos that cause malaria. The animator's ability to demonstrate such techniques in an easy-to-understand format arguably provided major grounds for efforts to get rid of such pests and opened up larger areas for human settlement.

The Rise of Television

After the war drew to a close, the studio and Walt Disney found themselves in a period of artistic and personal doldrums. Disney no longer felt quite the same drive that had fueled his creative, frenetic energy in his twenties. War contracts gave way to peace, and with it came no more direct work for the studio from the government. Not only did the end of the war leave the studio without contracts to do either animation or live-action films, but wartime also brought more public attention to other studios, which were becoming major players in the world of animated productions. Disney's competitors were catching up. They were doing animation features at lower cost and, according to many critics, producing quality that was just as good as (if not better than) the original Disney films. Competition led Disney to draw back from his animation work even more. The Golden Age of animation, an age that Disney and his studio animators had essentially created on their own and then set in motion, was over. For a while, it looked as if Disney Bros. was simply a product of that time and destined to be nothing more. Several factors changed this path and the history of American and global entertainment.

Between 1946 and 1950, Disney studios released three long features. These were no more than a hodgepodge of smaller animation shorts, cobbled together like a poorly made patchwork quilt. The studio also released a movie that would drown Disney in unwanted but hugely deserved racial animus. Animation was still so expensive that it was now frequently combined with live-action sequences that were far less costly to film. However, this was not what people had come to expect from Disney. Animation segments within the films like *Mickey and the Beanstalk* did not capture the attention of audiences or critics. Both saw such efforts as essentially warmed-over ideas, with little liveliness or originality. In 1946, the studio released the long-form film *Song of the South* with animation and live action. Based on folktales that portrayed the world of the Reconstruction-era South through the eyes of African Americans, the film was slammed by the National Association for the Advancement of Colored People (NAACP) for presenting insulting and demeaning stereotypes. But these protests were largely ignored in segregated white communities, where the film was greeted as just another Disney film. *Song of the South* was a modest success at the box office, and its cheery theme song, "Zip-a-Dee-Do-Dah," netted the studio an Oscar in 1948 for Best Song.

Searching for new ideas to bring to the big screen, Walt Disney stumbled on what would eventually become the genesis of the modern wildlife documentary. A husband-and-wife team spent months filming real-life scenes in Alaska. The footage they took of fur seals on the Pribilof Islands was the part of their work that Disney found most absorbing. He turned this venture into a documentary short called *Seal Island*. When RKO balked at distributing it on the grounds that no one was interested in the material, Disney made the decision to show the footage in a theater for a single week. Doing so qualified it for the Oscars. The eventual Oscar for Documentary Short Subject that *Seal Island* won began a revolution. At $86,000, it was a bargain to produce and a huge hit with audiences, earning over four times the cost of the initial expedition. Disney dubbed similar films that followed his "True-Life Adventure" series. From 1948 to 1960, the studio created 14 additional nature documentaries. Each film had a narrative imparting human emotions to wild animals, as well as a song track that was created after the film and was edited in-house. While they earned him even more Oscars, the films also led to allegations that Disney was taking nature and turning it into bland pabulum. Critics argued he was using a glossy face and easy framing instead of the complexity and accuracy required to show the real world.

Criticism like this highlights an issue that many modern documentary filmmakers must face when making films about the natural world. Most of the techniques that Disney Studios used have become a standard part of the arsenal used in wildlife documentaries. Close-ups of wild animals combined with an overarching narration of each scene are the kind of approach that viewers have come to expect in any wildlife film. The same principles apply whether watching the images at home or on huge IMAX screens, unfurling majestically. Filmmakers are still caught between telling the audience a story and simply letting nature do it for them. Such story-framing elements that Disney nature documentaries introduced to this genre can be seen in nature documentaries made decades after the original. The intense realism of the 2005 documentary *March of the Penguins* has much in common with the first nature documentary that Disney made, as filmmakers strive to help people understand what they are seeing on screen.

Live-action films without any animation continued to be a major source of revenue for the studio. The release of the all-live-action *Treasure Island* in 1950 earned the studio a large profit. In a very real sense, live-action films came to serve as a source of funding for the company's animation films in the coming years. Despite enormous successes, even two decades after it was founded and after incredible acclaim, the studio continued to lurch from picture to picture, facing the sincere and terrifying possibility of bankruptcy with every single production. In 1950, *Cinderella*, the studio's first animated feature since *Bambi* that was not a pastiche of other work, came to the screen after years of development. This film simply had to succeed, or else the company would have another bankruptcy on its hands and its work as a viable studio would end. Fortunately, the film was a hit both critically and at the box office, where it earned a hefty sum. While not necessarily advancing the art of animation in any substantially innovative way, the picture did ensure that the studio would remain a viable entity economically, still capable of bringing a story to the screen. The following years saw the release of several other animated features. Disney Studios released *Alice in Wonderland* in 1951. Making an animated feature from the famed Lewis Carroll book had been on Disney's mind since the beginning of his career. *Alice* was not a success either financially or with the critics. The storyline seemed contrived and confusing. The film was followed by *Peter Pan* in 1953, which was a moneymaker for the studio. *Lady and the Tramp* came along in 1955, another financial success even though it was excoriated by critics of the time for being overly sentimental.

While Disney Studios continued to churn out productions for the silver screen, another screen was getting equal attention from the public—and Walt and his brother too. Television proved to be just as much of a natural outlet for Disney's personality and vision as the decision to move to Los Angeles in his twenties had been. By the early 1950s, the number of Americans with access to television sets and the stations serving them began to grow quite briskly. Disney Studios actually applied to the government agency set up to monitor the airwaves, the Federal Communications Commission (FCC), for the right to run a television station at the end of World War II. Studio officials withdrew the application after thinking it over in more detail. Roy and Walt decided that it would be better to wait until color broadcasts were possible. The two brothers also believed, unlike so many of the other movie studio heads, that rather than being a threat to movies, television could act in tandem and bring in more revenue and greater exposure for the company's library of films. In 1950, NBC aired a Christmas broadcast featuring Walt Disney, along with cartoons and scenes from the upcoming release of *Alice in Wonderland*. The Disney brothers turned out to be exactly right: by 1953, two-thirds of all American households had a television set.

This was an astonishing transformation that would essentially change American social life in the same way that the Internet would decades later. Newly formed national networks were eager for programming to feed to their audiences. Walt Disney had a well-known name with instant appeal. The network heads sought him out personally. He wanted money to finance an innovative idea: a modern version of the classic theme park. What would become Disneyland was beginning to occupy most of his waking hours, with the kind of feverish intensity he hadn't felt in years. Disney struck a deal with ABC. As the smallest of the growing national networks, company officials preferred to find programming from already successful entertainment venues rather than spend money financing original work. He agreed to a three-year contract to create 26 one-hour programs a year for the network. Disney's wholesale embrace of this new technology was a radical move that had been spurned by every other motion picture studio. Doing so would prove to be an act of incredible prescience on Disney's part, and one that made him an indelible part of the new medium.

Part of Disney's innate talent was a complete willingness to find possibilities in almost any new technology far before others in his field got on board. Just as he had seen that sound and color would transform the animation field, he saw the same incredible possibilities in the power of the small screen. Television programming would ultimately save the studio financially, provide the funding he wanted for his amusement park, and bring his name and work to a whole new generation of fans. He used his new platform to promote his park for the remainder of his life, with the willing assent of ABC network officials. Disney also used it to bring attention to other ideas that briefly caught his attention. Walt had occasionally appeared in movies before and had been voicing Mickey Mouse for decades. The new medium brought him back to the studio again, and into the public's eye, in a weekly program that began in 1954. Initially called *Disneyland*, its name was changed to *Walt Disney Presents* in 1958. This was the springboard for the next, last, and perhaps most successful stage of his career. In his role as the host of his own television show, Disney was Uncle Walt, a genial man who spoke to families and children once a week. He was the voice of Everyman, at once confident and folksy, and yet, like most people, just a bit shy on camera. His detractors felt he was an exceptionally successful elitist pretending to be no more than a modest, local man of the people. While he was rich, famous, and one of the most accomplished and acclaimed men of his day, Disney's blue-collar roots were undeniably real. He came from a family where fiscal struggle was the order of the day. His early responsibility for the family paper route took him out of school and stunted his chances to explore the wider world around him. Disney never forgot the poverty that had marked his youth or his lack of education beyond a single year of high school and the way that it limited some of his horizons. As an all-American success story with that kind of background, he invited others to see themselves in his life and imagine that they might follow their own personal goals no matter where they led. Americans loved him for it.

The show on ABC was a massive, immediate hit with the public and advertisers. ABC officials gave him a format that essentially allowed the studio and Disney to do whatever they liked once a week. Their first success came from the very first television miniseries in 1954. Three episodes showing the life of Davy Crockett hit the airwaves and pop culture in a way that studio officials had not seen since the days of *Steamboat Willie*. A total of 40 million Americans out of a population of 163 million turned in, making it a seminal event in American pop culture history. Disney and ABC officials realized that parents would happily sit with their children to watch television together as a family. Once again, Disney refused to cut corners, so it was a lush production filmed on location. The studio's budget for the series was twice what ABC paid for the final product. Company officials more than recouped the cost when the series was released in movie theaters. This proved to Disney staffers that television could act as a catalyst for the studio's big-screen plans.

Other shows would have an equally important impact in different ways. Another miniseries, *Man in Space*, came about after Walt Disney read a magazine article about the possibilities of space exploration. Millions watched it in 1955; President Dwight D. Eisenhower was one of them. *Man in Space* arguably sparked the American passion for space that would culminate in the 1969 moon landing four years after Disney died. Disney did the same with a program called *Our Friend the Atom*. Here, the intention was to show the potential power of nuclear energy. As he had done for the nature documentary, the same transformational process was in play. Disney was one of the loudest and undeniably most influential Americans. The world listened to him when it came to thinking about the use of technology and science in their own lives.

Walt Disney Presents remained on television in one version or another until 1983. When the show moved to Sunday nights, it defined that time just before children went off to bed to face the start of the school week. Many parents and kids gathered in front of their sets to watch the latest Disney offering together. The program brought dozens of ideas over the years to the American public. And yet for Walt Disney, the show had largely one purpose: to serve as the primary basis for funding his vacation park and showing it off to the American public. This idea turned out to be his last act. His park would radically change the notion of the American amusement park. After his death, his brother Roy would push Walt Disney World into being in memory of his younger brother. In doing so, he turned Florida into such a tremendously different place that the state's history can be divided into the pre– and post–Walt Disney World eras. With help from financing via ABC and the massive audience it gave him, Disney was able to take that idea, flesh it out, and create a park that is still evolving today. The early years of the history of American television and the history of Disney and Disneyland are intertwined.

Creating Theme Parks

Throughout his life, Walt Disney was driven by many ideas. A whole slew of them almost magically turned into reality under his direction. As a young man, he looked to animation as a source of dreams and a potential career. Running off to Los Angeles in his early twenties, he shrugged off a prior bankruptcy to start a studio that brought color and sound to what had been an almost static, black-and-white, silent art form. Films like *Bambi* and *Alice in Wonderland* were artistically impressive, but a significant number of others were fiscal disasters. Walt still kept the studio going, even as the company faltered time and again. Creating new films was his motivation and the motivation that he conveyed to everyone he worked with. In his fifties, a single idea began to grip him in the same way that the concept of animation had many years earlier. His amusement park took the very notion of an amusement park and turned it inside out. While he faced both criticism and intense acclaim, the park would be his own private, and yet public retreat where he felt truly at home.

Amusement parks began as the concept of an outdoor garden where people could go in their free time after religious services or during their rare days off. Such gardens later evolved to include rides that charmed adults and children. In the 1950s, Disney seized on this idea and imagined it again. For him, his television show would go hand in hand with the idea of crafting a park that he rather egotistically dubbed *Disneyland*. Still playing a role in the overall running of Disney Studios, the park consumed his mind the same way that *Snow White* had pulled him into a vortex of concentrated intensity. He knew that he had to prove himself again to audiences, other studio executives, and fiscal backers. That prospect delighted him.

Work on the park in Southern California began in 1954, with plans to open a year later. Disneyland had a lot in common with most of Walt Disney's work in the past. Just as he had spent days poring over the little details in *Bambi*, he walked through each part of the land dedicated to Disneyland in person before guests showed up, looking at it with a critical eye. Like his other major enterprises, it had flaws he disliked intensely that were often only visible to those who really looked for them. Plans for certain areas were left unfinished because there wasn't quite enough money. Once again, he made little effort to pay attention to finances. The ideas in his head were all about the creation of quality spaces. He aimed to make Disneyland a much different place than other parks in existence at that time.

The same imperious quality that Disney brought when closely supervising films at the studio came out again. He may have been Walt at the studio, but not in California. Disney barked orders at workers to the point where they went on a brief strike. As he had done when creating his early movies, he even established an outlet to train workers for the work he wanted done. Disney University taught employees to exude the kind of essentially cheery disposition that later became the required code of conduct for workers. Like so many of his ideas, costs spiraled once it came to the final product. Just getting to opening day compelled him to find $17 million. Between investments from ABC and outside corporate sponsors, Disney barely managed to pull it off.

Disneyland was Walt's Disney's final act. Opening day was the pinnacle of his life and a chance to remake his childhood once again for the public. Here, he could reimagine American life as he truly wanted it and get rid of the nagging little dark corners that haunted him even as a hugely successful adult. The streets were swept clean to the point of obsession. Not a hint of dirt would mar his brand new world. For once, he could exert total control over something. He could take his flawed Kansas City life, full of painful memories, and erase it in favor of a shiny new Main Street. In the process, for the first time since *Snow White* so many years before, Disney Studios was back in the black.

The expansion and running of the park, along with his work on television, took much of his attention in the last decade of his life. He even had an apartment in the center of it all, where he could watch people enjoying his work. The idea for a second park in Florida began to take hold, as it was clear that Disneyland was going to be a huge hit financially. That was not to happen under his personal supervision. While Disney was generally a very healthy man with only minor ailments, he was also a heavy smoker. At sixty-five, it all caught up with him. Less than two months after being diagnosed with lung cancer, America's favorite uncle was dead.

The man from Chicago, Marceline, Kansas City, and Los Angeles was cremated as millions mourned. Uncle Walt brought Americans through the Great Depression, to World War II, and then into the 1950s and the turbulent 1960s. He was an American original, lauded all over the globe for his ability to make people laugh and shape how they thought about the world. Critics may have rightfully carped that he candy-coated everything along the way and sanitized it. They understandably argued that he ignored the less pleasant aspects of reality and the authentic pain of childhood in favor of the simple, even the simplistic. Yet the American public and much of the world remained on his side for most of his life.

The list of his accomplishments made Walt Disney a legendary part of American culture. Ranging from the creation of the first animated feature with color and synchronized sound to what would become years of innovation in filmmaking, his is a legacy impossible to ignore when talking about American culture. His television show also began the process of turning Americans' attention skyward well before Sputnik first launched. His work brought him a great deal of celebrity and tremendous personal satisfaction, as well as a platform for self-expression and ultimately fiscal stability.

At the end of his life, Disney had a shelf full of high industry honors and a large park with his name on it. History would see him as a restless person who found inspiration in big ideas and made them come alive. In the aftermath of his death, his eponymous company found similar highs and similar issues. Disney himself did much to remake parts of American life and change how Americans thought about themselves. His passage marked the first half of the Disney story, but there was much to come. The company's impact on the United States and the world, while not quite as direct as that of its founder, continues to play a role in the formation of America's image at home and across the globe.

Since His Death

At the time of his death, Walt Disney had been famous for decades. His death was relatively sudden. Few preparations were in place to respond after his quick, two-month battle with lung cancer. Walt left behind a group of ideas, with little instruction as to how to carry them out. Some of his concepts would be ignored as impractical or (ironically) not part of the Disney brand. A surprising number, however, continued to influence the path of the company in the coming decades. Over the years, Walt Disney involved several other family members in the direct running of Disney Studios. His two children, Diane and Sharon, were occasionally asked to provide opinions about various film projects. However, while he was an involved and loving father, he was also a product of his time when it came to women's role in the business sphere. His daughters were given money from the company and a chance to be with their father and share in many fun events, but little say in how it was run. The same was true of his wife. She was a silent partner who occasionally offered him the grounding that he needed to stay in touch with the average person's viewpoint. Lillian Disney did not share his fervor for works like *Snow White,* which she thought would be a failure. She felt the same sense of doom about his plans for an amusement park. Lillian Disney did not like being on display with her husband, even though she enjoyed the exciting life he gave her. It was not until 1987, when she pledged $50 million toward the construction of Walt Disney Concert Hall in Los Angeles, that she found any public role of her own. Designed by the modernist architect Frank Gehry and opened in 2003, the hall is a landmark that has had an impact on the creation of other American entertainment venues.

For the next five years after Walt's death, his older brother Roy took the helm. Roy lacked Walt's creative flair, but in his own way, he was just as dogged. Roy was very much a conventional man. His own steel came out after Walt died. Roy's complete determination in the years after Walt's death was the push behind bringing Disney World to life. In truth, his younger brother often baffled him. Walt's single-minded pursuit of ideas that did not seem possible deeply confused his nearest-in-age elder brother. When it all came together, Roy was there to take a cold, hard look at the finances. He was the one person whom Walt trusted for years to figure out how to find the monetary safety nets to make it all work somehow, even in the face of looming bankruptcy. After his brother died, Roy wanted to retire. Disney was finally in the black and apparently set to remain there for the foreseeable future. But this was not to be. Roy's primary task in the next five years, as he saw it, was bringing Disney World into being in his brother's name. This meant achieving two goals: persuading the government to let him run the lands they'd purchased with special legal provisions and finding yet more financing for yet another incredibly large-scale project. Roy Disney was a relatively modest man, and he knew this. His brother's films were largely Walt's creation, with little input from Roy in any meaningful creative way. What would be Roy's contribution, in many ways, was Disney World. The park was to be his personal homage to his brother and the final act of his life.

Roy Disney died a short time after Walt Disney World opened in 1971. The park flourished. Despite the fact that bringing it to life cost over $400 million, it was readily apparent that this was money well spent. Walt had been right about the appeal of a second park. In the first two years alone, 20 million people came to Orlando. Over the next decade, studio executives expanded into several new ventures. They bought up more land, developed the existing acres, and opened three new theme parks. Epcot, Disney's Hollywood Studios, and Disney's Animal Kingdom made the 1980s a busy time for the park's creative directors.

New attractions remain on the horizon at every turn, as the park's top brass look for ways to bring in innovative concepts to the public. The same would hold true for Disneyland. Original rides, shows, and attractions continued to bring in visitors eager to see the latest Disney attraction, even when they've been to the park a dozen times before. Disney officials also found a home for Disney parks in other parts of the world. This would have pleased Walt Disney immensely, as he viewed himself in part as an ambassador from the United States to the rest of the world.

Disneyland and Disney World were enormous financial and critical successes. Much of the company's creative energies found an outlet in the parks, with rides and shows that expanded the Disney brand in new directions. Unfortunately, the same could not be said for Disney films during this period. Films that had once captured the attention of people everywhere limped along for years after the opening of Disney World. It was not until an inventive revival in the mid-1980s that the film division would again show the kind of spark and imagination that had so entranced the public five decades before. Company officials seemed determined to cling to historic laurels rather than explore the world of film in the way that Disney had during his tenure. Releasing old features again became a staple company policy. Dubbed the "Disney Vault" at the company, the policy of releasing such features every 10 years again drew fantastic revenues, but little else. *Snow White* was released eight times, bringing in over $50 million at the box office. *Beauty and the Beast* has been rereleased three times after it was first shown in theaters in 1991. The same process continued for many years until the creation of Disney+ promised to put an end to it.

In the mid-1980s, studio officials spun off a brand new venture. Touchstone Pictures was based on the idea that Disney might play a role in the film industry in a different way. This was about tapping into a more risqué market while keeping Disney's more family-friendly films separate. The mostly live-action films were a series of hits. Films such as *Splash*, *Down and Out in Beverly Hills*, and *Good Morning, Vietnam* showed versatility despite the occasional dud and brought in adult audiences before the studio was absorbed into Disney in 2016. Studio officials also began a return to their animation roots. New technology made it easier to produce animated features at far less cost. Animated hits like *The Lion King* and *Mulan* made it clear that Disney was once again a major player in the world of animation. In the coming years, the studio further expanded into other ventures, including Broadway productions, a cruise line, and stores selling Disney merchandise in malls all over the country.

What was once a simple idea in the teenaged Walt's brain about having fun telling stories now reaches into many facets of American life. In the 1920s, the company changed the world of animation. In the 1930s, the same company changed the world of American movies. As America entered World War II, the studio was there to help. They served the American public with films that were sometimes propaganda and sometimes a means of riding communities of pest infestation. Disney was even instrumental in pushing the president of the United States to literally conduct the process of war differently. The company dove right into the war effort and was rewarded in turn with an image that linked it with patriotism in the public mind.

After the war, the decade that followed saw both triumph and controversy. Television proved to be yet another incredibly successful medium for the studio, and one that afforded the company the funding to create what is arguably the world's most successful amusement park. Episodes from the company's television show played a major hand in creating everything from the start of the space race to the idea of the nature documentary.

At the same time, Disney's increasing conservatism led him to side with regressive McCarthyism and may have contributed to the studio's decision to bring movies dripping with racism to the big screen. Workers often struggled to bring his ideas to life while being denied opportunities to take credit or decent wages. In the aftermath of his death, his brother Roy used the idea and creation of Disney World to make Orlando a different place and turn Florida into a worldwide vacation destination.

Since then, while the company no longer has the immediate ear of the president, it continues to play an outsized role in how Americans think of themselves and how the world thinks of America. Disney's vision may have been flawed, occasionally lapsing into needless sentiment and facile platitudes. Disney's story is one that his biographers admit sometimes glossed over the truth of the little details of his life and embellished them into a series of more interesting narratives because Walt Disney loved a good story. However, the imaginative power of the company and incredible, remarkable innovations pushed by one determined man from Chicago cannot ultimately be denied or ignored.

CHAPTER TWO

From Steamboat Willie to Buzz Lightyear: Disney and the Establishment of the American Animation Industry

When most people think of the impact that Disney Studios has had on the world, it all begins with animation. Walt Disney may have changed the very idea of animation forever, but he was not the first person to dream of a series of drawings that moved. Taking a series of figures and making them shift in the light creates an ideal that human beings have been attempting to bring to life for millennia. Artists have always aimed to translate live movement onto the confines of flat surfaces. Paintings on ancient cave walls dating almost to the beginnings of human history show artists drawing horses moving across the walls in a way that modern animators would easily recognize. Cultures as different as the Romans, medieval Italy, and ancient China all had some version of this concept. Each was home to people who found ways to bring it alive in rudimentary form. All these concepts remained static until a few ideas began to transform the very notion of art. These ideas would lead to the world that Walt Disney later made his own and turned into something entirely different.

Animation before Disney

The first invention that changed the world of moving pictures was photography. Cameras ended the need to spend hours painting just to capture a single image. Photography stems from the idea of what is known as the "camera obscura," a box that projects an image on the wall that can then be traced. Artists used it for centuries as a guide to creating realistic images on surfaces. The camera obscura did not capture actual images that could be replicated on other surfaces. The mechanism provided a means of bringing art to life and let each individual artist offer a personal interpretation of the projected image. Over time, this device gradually became small enough to be portable via the use of the developing technology of finely focused ground lenses. The camera obscura began to turn into the modern version about two hundred years ago. From the 1830s until the 1860s, artists experimented with many types of chemicals on many kinds of metals. They hoped to bring photography into a modern era that they could only dimly realize at the time. The goal was an image that accurately reflected reality and remained in place permanently. The new camera not only worked much better than expected, but it also became cheaper, to the point where many people of ordinary means could afford them. Experimentation led to the creation of a device known as the "zoetrope," which allowed the viewer to move a series of pictures rapidly and make it look as though an object were in motion. Photographer Eadweard Muybridge set out to prove a bet in the 1870s that all four of a horse's hooves would remain off the ground at some point in time. His work in settling this question brought him much acclaim and attention, as well as setting the stage for the idea of animation via the use of cameras. The next twenty years saw the development of the first movie camera and a transformation of the ideas behind the camera into live, working models. American inventor Thomas Edison pounced on this idea. He and his team in New York created a flexible series of pictures that could be pulled along quickly to create the feeling of movement for the viewer. By 1894, the first movie theater opened in New York City to popular acclaim and extreme curiosity. Edison was joined in the process by many others looking to make money. They came up with new ideas that sought to advance the groundwork for this medium in new ways. In France, the Lumière brothers, Auguste and Louis, spent several years working on their own version of a portable movie camera. The two would go on to develop the "first successful photographic colour process" by 1907 and have their work hailed all over the world. They were part of a world that included innovators such as the Frenchman Émile Reynaud. His Théâtre Optique of 1888 used a simple series of very slowly moving, hand-painted images to create films lasting 10 to 15 minutes.

Modern animation developed along a similar path in tandem with many developments in the cinematic world. A device known as a "magic lantern" allowed users to project a series of images in a quick pattern against a surface as early as the 18th century. Lighting methods of the day were weak, making it mostly a toy for upper-class amusement with little practical application. It was not until the creation of light that came from burning limestone with other chemicals that the lantern and other techniques started to attract real attention from people in many fields. These proved popular with crowds all over Europe and the Americas in the 19th century. However, this particular technique, a novelty that led to the first use of the phrase "in the limelight," was very dangerous. Explosions were common. The Belgian physicist and mathematician Joseph Plateau created a device that he called the "Phenakistiscope" in 1832. The machine, a precursor to the modern Graphics Interface Format (GIF) technology, allowed the user to create fluid motion from a series of images that could be moved very quickly. While it may seem as if the flip book, in which many pages are moved quickly to make it appear as if the drawings inside are moving, is a modern invention, it too has deep roots in the 19th century. Called the Kineograph, it was patented by British printer John Barnes Linnett. Animation was seen as an amusing parlor trick and little else. In the United States, several pioneers stepped up, along with Edison, to bring Americans access to animation. The illustrator James Stuart Blackton was fascinated by this new art form. In 1906, he produced what might be considered the world's first animated movie produced directly on film. In *Humorous Phases of Funny Faces*, the artist drew several characters on a blackboard with chalk and then erased them. This was known as the "crank step technique." Crank step was crude, but it was effective and captured the attention of audiences all over the globe. As Donald Crafton points out in his book *Before Mickey: The Animated Film, 1898–1928*, his work and the work of others at this point was very much a vaudeville routine come to life.

In the next decade, animation underwent many new technological phases. During this time, it went from a simple idea to what was an essential part of the burgeoning movie industry. Characters like Felix the Cat and Gertie the Dinosaur were world famous long before Mickey Mouse arrived. Films like *Fantasmagorie*, the work of the French artist Émile Cohl, prefigured concepts that would loom large in many Disney films.

Technology started to transform the animation industry even further from 1910 to 1920. Pioneers who were willing to experiment created animation techniques that formed the basis of later efforts. Raoul Barré worked with Edison Studios. He developed a system on his own known as the "peg system," which allowed him to keep his drawings in place and made it possible to craft a broader storyline in less time. The idea was later refined further by Disney with the use of high-tech pegs. A second system, known as "slash and tear," made it possible to create animation even faster. This technique was popularly used until the creation of the cel system made it obsolete in the 1920s. Animators at the Barré Studio were lured away by higher salaries offered by another American mogul. William Randolph Hearst ran his International Film Service starting in 1914. While hugely influential for several years, the studio was disbanded seven years later, largely for being pro-German at the height of World War I. His emphasis on the use of cartoons translated well into existing ideas about animation. Hearst was joined by several other American animators who would turn the existing industry on its head. John Randolph Bray and Earl Hurd both filed for patents centered around the cel system that aimed to make animation faster, easier, and cheaper. Giannalberto Bendazzi states in his *Cartoons: One Hundred Years of Cinema Animation*, "Hurd's process was not only alternative, but ultimately more important than Bray's: it consisted of the cel process, involving the drawing of characters on transparent celluloid sheets, which then were applied over painted background scenes."

In 1915, fellow American Max Fleischer earned a patent for a technique known as "rotoscoping," which made it much easier to create much more realistic animation in which movement flowed from one instance to the next. Rotoscoping was widely used by the animation industry and remained a mainstay of movies until it was replaced by computer animation decades later. This period also saw the release of early animated films such as *Little Nemo* and *Gertie the Dinosaur*. These were the works of Winsor McCay, an illustrator famous for his comic strip, *Little Nemo in Slumberland*. Little Nemo is full of movement and personality. McCay's work can be seen as having the kind of viewpoint that Walt Disney wanted to bring to the screen when he developed Mickey Mouse. John Canemaker's *Winsor McCay: His Life and Art* points out that this film introduced many techniques that would become standard in the industry later, such as tracing paper, registration marks, and recycling drawings to make it easier to get the movement he wanted. He did not bother to patent his work, as he thought that it was so laborious, he did not imagine that anyone else might want to use it or that it might make a profit. It was left to Disney and others like Otto Messmer, Paul Terry, and Bill Nolan to step in and take these essential animation concepts even further.

Mickey, Minnie, and the Start of the Golden Age of Animation

While other parts of the country held promise, New York City was the center of the young world of animation. Home to many movie theaters, it offered a ready audience for animation products. Books like *Animated*

Cartoons: How They Are Made, Their Origin and Development by E. G. Lutz in 1920 publicized the brand-new directions that New Yorkers were bringing to this art and commercial form of entertainment. The book was in essence a how-to manual that drew on the short history of animation to date and showed readers they could make them at home. Disney devoured the book at his local library. His *Steamboat Willie* may appear to the casual viewer to come out of nowhere, but nothing could be further from the truth. It took him eight years to make the six-minute movie that would come along and sweep in a new era in filmmaking. Even with all his hard work, it took Disney a lot of time to break out of the straitjacket formulas that made many forms of early animation seem alike. Disney took such concepts and traveled along a path that ultimately led to *Snow White and the Seven Dwarfs*.

Fans know Mickey and Minnie. But it was a cat named Felix who came before them with an audience and a great many fans. Accounts differ as to who came up with the idea of Felix and his adventures. Some scholars credit the Australian-American cartoonist Patrick Sullivan with the original idea. His tiny New York studio created a series of shorts, including *The Tale of Thomas Kat* in 1917. Many others credit German-American animation pioneer Messmer, who worked in Sullivan's studio. He is seen as the animator responsible for Felix in the same way that Disney colleague Ub Iwerks played a huge role in the creation of Mickey Mouse. Messmer brought the character to life and made it his own. Starting in 1919, Felix the Cat was an instant hit with the public, just as Mickey would be a decade later. A total of 25 animated shorts were released to an adoring public between 1919 and 1921. Felix did dozens of humanlike activities. He went to war. He rallied the troops. He fell in love. He was a character constantly in motion, seeming to free himself from the constraints imposed by three-dimensional surfaces. In the 1920s, Felix was as much of a star as Charlie Chaplin. But there was one thing he didn't do: talk. While Messmer would turn the character into a cartoon, and others into a television series, his days as a movie pioneer were overtaken when a resolute young man named Walt Disney came along.

The twenty-year-old Walt was fascinated by the subject of animation. He produced his own shorts with a studio he called Laugh-O-Gram. Shown in movie theaters in Kansas City, these crude films were such a hit with locals that he became a minor celebrity in his own right well before the rest of the world would learn his name. The shorts that Disney created were based on fairy tales including *Little Red Riding Hood*, *Puss in Boots*, and *Goldilocks and the Three Bears*. Several animators came along for the ride with him at the time, including Friz Freleng and Rudolf Ising. The two did legendary animation work at Warner Bros. decades later. Unfortunately, the distributor paid them very little money up front and then went on to declare bankruptcy a short time later. When a local investor stepped up to offer the studio more money, Disney used those funds to create a project he called *Alice's Wonderland*. The combination of live action and animation would be mirrored much later in many films to come, such as *Mary Poppins*, but it was not enough to make the studio a success. Walt left for California with his reels in hand. Here, he found backers and continued his work on the *Alice* series. It was a commercial success.

Hot on the heels of Felix the Cat, Disney brazenly decided it was time to create his own version. Ub Iwerks came up with the idea of a cartoon rabbit. Oswald the Lucky Rabbit was said to be the cartoon version of actor Douglas Fairbanks. The character was obviously a blatant rip-off of Felix the Cat; he had the same overall look and a bendable body that was apparently capable of doing almost anything physically. Disney lost control of the character when Charles Mintz took over his studio in the late 1920s. Cartoons featuring Oswald continued production until 1943. The character was so integral to the studio's history that Disney chief executive officer (CEO) Robert Iger eventually finagled a way to get the rights back to Disney in 2006. Oswald allowed Walt Disney to set the stage for his next idea: Mickey Mouse.

Like many other aspects of early Disney history, the origins of Mickey Mouse are in slight dispute by historians. Walt Disney adored a good tale. He was not above taking his own work and embellishing it to make his background story more intriguing. What is known is that Ub Iwerks and Disney came up with the idea of the mouse after Disney lost control of Oswald the Lucky Rabbit. The real question was how Mickey came by his name. Disney told his audience that he'd originally wanted to call the mouse Mortimer, but his wife, Lillian, hated the name and lobbied for Mickey instead. Historians at the National Museum of American History believe that it is more likely that the two saw a popular toy with the name Mickey and liked the sound of "Mickey" better. This time, unlike Oswald, they immediately patented the name of their character so they could keep him. Mickey was the star of a short released in 1928 called *Plane Crazy*, and then in *The Gallopin' Gaucho*. The public didn't much like either movie, but Disney was sure he was on the right track. Mickey showed up next in *Steamboat Willie*. This short film was the vehicle the animator chose specifically to show off synchronized sound and the character he had in mind at the same time. The title and idea paid homage to *Steamboat Bill, Jr.* Buster Keaton's film was not a success at the time, but later would be seen as one of the masterpieces of the silent film era. Mickey was the first cartoon character to have a voice.

Disney was sure synchronized sound was the next step, and one that would put him above the competition. For the first time, sound wasn't simply an afterthought that had little to do with what was happening on screen. As Mickey moved, the sounds went with him. The quality of the sound was also crucial. Disney wanted the audience to hear the music and admire it almost as much as he wanted them to watch the cartoon. He hired a 17-piece orchestra to give depth to the images he was animating.

The initial results were terrible. Tinkering with a bouncing ball on the screen allowed the orchestra to keep time and make it work. Animation historians believe that Iwerks did most of the animation under Disney's direction. Before Mickey, there was little that set Disney apart from his competitors. Once *Steamboat Willie* opened, that all changed. According to the Museum of Modern Art, "The movie opened at New York's Colony Theater on November 18, 1928, a date that would become known as Mickey's birthday." A cold November day marked the first step of Disney's march to world fame and the beginning of the Golden Age of Animation.

Steamboat Willie was a rapturous hit with the public and saved Disney from fiscal ruin at the same time. The movie also saved animation. By this time, only about one in five movie theaters were willing to carry animated movies. For the first time, audiences were happy to sit through an entire movie just to see *Steamboat Willie* again. Many other studios did not agree with the new idea of synchronized sound and dismissed it outright. Felix the Cat was an international star with a huge following. The studio that owned him did not see how synchronized sound could make a difference and create intense audience interest. Rather than creating new cartoons using this technology, the creators of Felix simply added sound to previous cartoons the audience had already seen. It was too late. Audiences wanted Mickey and his brand-new ideas, not a remake of Felix.

The short allowed Disney to show off his imagination and exactly what the medium of animation might offer when it came to telling a story. Unlike working with live actors, he could use animation to bring movement to the screen in new ways and play around with the idea of on-screen movement itself. While the film was greeted happily, parents found Mickey more of a showoff than the benevolent figure he would later become. The Mickey of *Steamboat Willie* is full of mischief. He scampers around, unsupervised by adults. Most of his time is spent being mean to his fellow animals and avoiding work. He's also more rat than mouse, with his pointed nose and long tail. Minnie is there as well, as Mickey's obvious spouse, making it clear that this Mickey is a grown-up creation.

The character was not only a hit in the United States; he was also a hit with the rest of the world. In the next few years, Mickey appeared in dozens of films and came to embody the essence of what the world thought of an animated character. Gossip columnists called him a star in his own right. The 1930s can be described, as recent Disney biographer Neal Gabler suggests, as "the age of Mickey Mouse both for the way the mouse seemed to confront the period's dislocations and agonies and for the way he seemed to suggest a remedy for them." He was uncomplicated and made audiences happy. Mickey underwent a radical transformation that made him an entirely different creation from the mouse of *Steamboat Willie*. He was now a more juvenile mouse, with larger eyes, a rounded body, and a much smaller nose that spoke directly of childhood. He also lost much of his moxie. This was a mouse that confronted adversity and came out on top at every turn. His adventures were also of a much blander sort than his debut. Mickey was a mild-mannered creature who wouldn't dare confront his boss or upset the status quo. His transformation was akin to the journey that Disney took from cheeky outsider to the ultimate member of the club. He was portrayed in bright colors and then gradually faded into the background as other characters took over for him.

Disney brought his mouse to life only occasionally. His character served as a logo of sorts, to remind fans what Disney was doing during films such as *Fantasia,* where he was one of the hosts. With Mickey Mouse generating fans and creating revenue for the studio, it freed Disney to think about his next big adventure in the world of animation. *Snow White and the Seven Dwarfs* was to take over where Mickey left off. The full-length animated feature was his boldest venture, one that would define an era and change the world of animation permanently.

Walt's Folly: The Story of *Snow White and the Seven Dwarfs*

Mickey Mouse taught Disney and his animators that animation could be more than a series of coarse drawings. Finesse was the idea going forward. Mickey shorts were fine, but he wanted something a lot more. In 1933, Disney went in a new direction yet again with the release of *The Three Little Pigs*. The slightly longer film illustrated his overall approach to animation during the next few years. Color had long been a dream in the movie world. Technicolor was actually available as early as 1917, but at the time, it was not particularly elegant or especially accurate at conveying the depth of color that audiences and filmmakers wanted. It was also expensive. In the early 1930s, experimenters at Technicolor weren't quite ready to work in live-action films, where technical flaws would become easily visible. Animation seemed a more suitable outlet. Here, colors could be just a little bit off and audiences wouldn't care. Disney decided that the appeal of the color process might be just enough to convince studios to go with his animation shorts rather than those of his competitors. His current work with Mickey and the *Silly Symphonies* was successful but took months and longer to earn back the enormous sums spent to make them. Officials at Technicolor promised him exclusive access to their process. As would prove true with so many other forms of technological innovation, he readily embraced the opportunity. *The Three Little Pigs* was a hit. The short earned the studio an Oscar in 1934 and proved that Disney was right to embrace another new technological development. The film's theme song, "Who's Afraid of the Big Bad Wolf?" became an anthem of determination during the depths of the Great Depression. His next project would be even bigger and change animation forever.

The story of *Snow White* has ancient roots in many European countries. The concept that Disney drew on for his own version began as one of the many folk tales collected by the Brothers Grimm. Disney claimed to have seen a live-action version in the movies as a young man. Picking this particular story to bring to life appealed to him for many reasons. Animation historians pointed to the many elements that had parallels in his own life. There are cruel parents who do not care for the main character, lots of drudge work, and the end promise of a utopia when all is done. Historical accounts, like so many facts when it comes to writing about Disney and his plans, are not quite clear.

It is not known exactly when Disney began setting his plans in motion. Most historians agree that it was a three-year process that began about 1934. Walt Disney felt he had to stay in front of the competition to hold the audience's attention. His animators were so skeptical at first, they called it "Walt's Folly." Disney brought them in and acted out his plans for the movie, complete with sound and motion. To his audience of animators, it was clear it didn't matter what they thought about the whole thing—Disney was determined to bring it off.

There were quite a few obstacles in the way. The first was the reality of getting financing. Until the rise of computing power, animation was massively expensive. Even in the middle of the Great Depression, banks were not necessarily happy extending credit to Uncle Walt. The second was finding animators capable of following his instructions. Studio officials began an intensive drive to find animators who would be up to the immense task he had in mind. Disney sent a letter to art schools across the country. Thousands of people responded; Disney settled on 20 artists. Once on staff, the animators had to take weekly art classes as the picture progressed. Disney wanted animators who were dedicated not only to the ideal of excellence, but the total obsession he felt needed to go with it. No detail was too small to escape his notice. To study the physics of motion, his animators dropped rocks in water, slammed doors, and even threw bricks through plate glass windows and filmed it all. Everything in the film, including the rocks and trees, needed a purpose and a personality to go with it. In the original *Snow White*, the dwarves are interchangeable. They don't have personalities, or even names. Months were spent debating the names and characteristics of the characters we now know as Bashful, Doc, Dopey, Grumpy, Happy, Sleepy, and Sneezy. Disney hammered home to his animators that all of them needed to have individual feelings. He knew audiences could identify with each dwarf and advance the storyline at the same time. Major characters like the Queen were turned from a vague idea to a full-fledged vision with a voice and a point of view.

The work was so much in such a short time that Disney demanded 300 more animators as it started to come to life. Studio officials found another 22 to help with production. They did the vast grunt work required just to clean up after the initial cels were created. There were other parts of the feature that drew nearly equal attention from Disney. Music had to go along with the movie and make it all come together. He aimed for music that he deemed "quaint," rather than the more modern tunes others wanted. His goal was to create a musical distinction and songs that people could hum. Another aim was finding the right use of color. Disney believed that audiences expected bright colors when viewing cartoons. He wanted something more subtle. The colors in the final product are far more muted than in other, similar animation efforts. There's a real sense the audience is looking at a series of paintings come to life. All this perfectionism was extremely costly.

The final tally offers an impressive parade of numbers. Roughly 750 people worked on the film between first conception and the final picture. Disney started out by asking his investors for a budget of $250,000—an incredible sum when the average annual American income of the time was just over $1,300. By the time it was finished, the true costs were estimated at about $1.5 million. In comparison, a typical Disney short cost $25,000 to make, and live-action films of the day usually had a budget of about half that. Almost 2 million individually hand-painted cels went into the making of the film.

Despite all the passion and effort put into creating *Snow White and the Seven Dwarfs*, Disney wasn't entirely pleased with the results. Later, he would point out all the flaws in the movie and think about making it all over again with improved technology. Audiences and critics overlooked any problems and adored every moment. The December 21, 1937, world premiere was marked by gushing from world-famous industry officials. Charlie Chaplin said of *Snow White* that it "even surpassed our highest expectations." Within weeks, there were long lines at the box office waiting to see his next big adventure. *Snow White* wound up earning back the huge costs required to make it happen and more.

The film was and remains profoundly popular for a great many reasons. The simple storyline made it easy to follow. Each dwarf has an understandable and relatable personality. Animators used the dwarves to advance the plot. Disney's insight that minor characters could play a role in the film's progression charmed audiences. The movie's light gags made viewers laugh. The poignant scene where Grumpy breaks down and cries when he finds Snow White after she has bitten into the poisonous apple and fallen into a coma humanized him and added poignancy. With this film, Disney took animation from a series of comedic shorts that symbolized little in the public mind to the realm of full-fledged storytelling. In 1994, decades after the picture was first released, it sold 17 million copies in three weeks when released on home video. Disney Studios made a daring leap into the void and came out on top. This was the obvious next stage in animation. Over the following decade, his company brought to life some of the most beloved animated films of all time.

For Disney, *Snow White* ultimately accomplished one specific goal: to prove to himself and the world that the full-scale animation process he had in mind for a feature-length film was actually technologically possible. *Snow White* was the first of five films that marked the start of the Golden Age of Animation. Disney and his artists set the standards for animation and redefined the genre for audiences all over the world. Four additional movies, *Pinocchio, Fantasia, Dumbo,* and *Bambi,* place Disney as the single most influential purveyor of American animation of the 20th century. These films are artistic landmarks that parents and children alike continue to watch. *Dumbo* was the only film both admired by the critics and capable of earning back the money it cost to make at the box office.

Disney was not the only company creating American animation. During this period, others left his studio for the chance to take advantage of the technology that Disney had pioneered. The company's biggest rival in the global animation market was Warner Bros., which had a unique take on the art form that served in direct contrast to Disney's conception of the purpose of animation. Walt's emphasis was on beauty and bringing the natural world to the big screen. Warner Bros. went in an entirely different direction, making films with a certain subversive quality that the earnest Disney lost after the insouciant Mickey of *Steamboat Willie* became a placid puffball. Their cartoons harked directly back to the vaudeville origins of animation in a way that Disney had largely abandoned. Unlike Disney's productions, the shorts from Warner Bros. did not necessarily seek to expand the artistry of animation. What that studio did was to grab the audience's attention and reveal that it was possible for studios other than Disney to make animated features worth watching.

Characters from the *Looney Tunes* series, like Elmer Fudd, Daffy Duck, and Bugs Bunny, like the original Mickey Mouse, had the same kind of nonchalant and mocking quality that Mickey had originally had. They offered a brash take on the American worldview. The films were equally popular with adults. Tex Avery at Warner Bros. and other animators at smaller studios developed ideas that went in a different direction than the verisimilitude and elegance that Disney always pushed for his crop of animators. Cartoon physics let the animators play with the medium in a new way. Here, characters ignored the constraints of the physical world. Gravity and perspective were always skewed, and the fourth wall was often ignored as characters invited the audience to join them in celebration.

In 1940, the MGM feature *The Milky Way* was the first animated feature not by Disney to win the Oscar for Best Animated Short Film. MGM continued to provide audiences with an alternative to Disney in the upcoming decades. Their *Tom and Jerry* series by animators William Hanna and Joseph Barbera earned seven Oscars with a style that emphasized vivid violence and constant on-screen gore.

The Xerography Process

In the next decade, Disney and his animators brought out animated features that were noted for many reasons. Each second on screen was intended to be a doorway into a magical world where loveliness and intricate detail was a primary consideration. This kind of animation remained as expensive as ever, even years after *Snow White*. The films that the studio made from the 1930s to the 1950s continued to aim for the high bar Disney had set with his first film. Their work was an exhaustive process that did not always lead to financial success. Disney movies may have been widely admired by critics, but more than half were outright fiscal failures. *Alice in Wonderland* and *Lady and the Tramp* were moderate hits at the box office but frustrating to craft. Months were spent on individual scenes and plotlines that Disney might choose to discard because he didn't like the results. *Sleeping Beauty* took six years just to get to perfection by the time of its release in 1959 and then earned very little at the box office.

Disney remained committed to the animation process. Other officials at his studio realized that the company had to find ways to cut costs or else bankruptcy was a real possibility no matter what they did. Disneyland was a terrifically profitable venture, but the animation studios at Disney dealt with constant layoffs. Roy Disney wanted to shut them down completely in favor of television production. Salvation for the company's animation division came in the form of a new process and a new direction. Gone were the fairy tales imported from Europe. Gone too were the hours of hand-painting involved to create each cel and the incredible labor costs. All the previous films that the studio brought to the public were literally made by hand, as each image the public saw came from the work of skilled artists devoted to their craft. The humble Xerox machine set this process in motion and transformed the animation process. The results may have been cheaper, and therefore faster and easier, but they also lacked the kind of quality that Disney had made his own. Audiences and critics alike noticed the difference.

No one had to paint cels any longer. Instead, the new technology meant that all the art was scanned directly on top of the cellular material. The first Disney film to use this concept was *One Hundred and One Dalmatians*. The film, released in 1961, was a turn away from princesses and castles in favor of modern settings and characters. Whereas the need to paint every single Dalmatian might have been daunting in the past, the xerography process, where copies could be made rapidly, meant that the studio did not have to spend hours, months, or even years animating every single one of the 101 Dalmatians. Walt Disney was not especially fond of this method. He felt that it took some of the wizardry out of animation. But he also realized that it freed the company from the enormous costs that threatened to shut down his studio entirely.

In a real sense, the xerography process also liberated the studio from the fundamental vision that Walt Disney had offered the world. He wanted animation to rise above its crude origins and aspire to art. *Sleeping Beauty* was the apotheosis of animation as an artistic venture under Disney's supervision, and the culmination of all his ideas of what an animated feature should look like. The film has incredible artistic details that Disney could only dream of bringing to life when he first started to plan *Snow White*. Each cel has the feel of a painting and uses a vast array of marvelous colors. There are no such intricate details in *One Hundred and One Dalmatians*. The backdrop is flat and lacks any attempt to portray three dimensions.

One Hundred and One Dalmatians marked the start of a new era for the studio. For the first time, costs were reined in and kept that way. It also marked an end to the kind of acclaim the studio had regularly been earning from euphoric critics. Nevertheless, *One Hundred and One Dalmatians* was a fiscal hit with audiences and earned good reviews. It also marked a slide from the artistic heights Disney had pulled off during the Golden Age of Animation. For roughly the next three decades, the animated films they brought to the screen were simply not as popular with audiences. They were equally unpopular with critics who were used to Disney setting the highest possible standards for any animated feature. The xerography process would rescue the art form in a sense by making animation features possible on a budget, but it also sacrificed much along the way. Only a daring newcomer and a revolutionary new way of making animation would bring back the company's original glow and finally restore Disney's artistic reputation.

After Walt Disney died, his brother Roy officially took over. The majority of his time was devoted to the creation of Disney World in Orlando. When Roy died, he was followed by Ron Miller, Disney's son-in-law. He took over from his wife's uncle, Roy Disney. The next three decades saw a series of films that have at best a collective reputation for mediocrity. Disney Studios churned out films that didn't do much more than satisfy audiences and create the occasional memorable scene and song. Studio officials weren't quite sure what they wanted, beyond pleasing audiences and earning money. The older animators who had put life into Walt's very gestures headed off to retirement, and the group that Disney had jokingly called his Nine Old Men (in homage to President Franklin D. Roosevelt's mockery of the nine judges on the Supreme Court) was relegated to animation history. These were the men he hired in the mid-1930s, when Disney was getting *Snow White* in place. They were the animators who created the style for each Disney film. Their painstaking devotion to quality was now seen as old-fashioned and out of touch with the wants of the contemporary American public.

The xerography process led to films rife with heavy black lines, bright primary colors, and passive, static backdrops. Such efforts lacked the feel of entering an entirely new world that Disney had made his own. These films were ordinary. They adhered to a basic formula and did not take the kind of risks that Disney had routinely made part of his business culture. The limited technology meant that the films all tended to look alike. Gone were Disney's famous history of meticulousness and marvelously intricate detail. Critics dubbed features like *The Many Adventures of Winnie the Pooh* and *The Great Mouse Detective* scratchy. The graininess apparent in each one mimicked the look of doodles scratched out by someone with little talent, in their spare time.

Disney Studios also suffered from the loss of new and truly top animators who would go on to do great work in their own right. Don Bluth left in 1979, taking many top animators with him. For the next decade, Bluth remained the studio's most imaginative competitor and much praised by critics. His were films with a dark bent that Disney largely shunned. Efforts in the 1980s like *The Secret of NIMH* and *An American Tail* offered brand-new forms of realism and an American setting that Disney had not explored in any depth. By the late 1980s and beyond, new ideas and energy had returned the studio to its original prominence as the premier American animation studio. Once again, people looked to Disney not only for lush animation, but for well-told stories and memorable music.

Disney's Renaissance period spanned roughly the entire 1990s. Nearly every year saw the release of films that drew audiences back to the studio's releases and delighted them yet again. Unlike previous decades, when it took six years just to get *Sleeping Beauty* completed, the new films came out at a swift pace. More important, they were often successful at the box office. Critics were once again at Disney's feet, waiting to see what the studio would do next.

Several features can be said to characterize this period. For the first time in decades, Disney animators were encouraged to experiment and look at varied sources for imaginative inspiration, such as Greek and Chinese myths, rather than simple fairy tales. Heroines were no longer blank ciphers but rather fully fleshed-out characters. Belle from *Beauty and the Beast* manages to transcend the vapid princesses that were a staple of previous efforts. She's an unashamed bookworm and a spirited young woman. The same is true of *Mulan*. Viewers are given a bold female lead who is unafraid to step up to the plate and lead her community, even if she has to pretend to be a man to do it.

These films took audiences all over the world. *The Lion King* is set in Africa. *Pocahontas* takes place in colonial America, and *The Hunchback of Notre Dame* in Paris. Legendary songwriters like Howard Ashman and Alan Menken offered the kind of hummable songs that had not been part of Disney's movies for years. Near-constant triumphs for the studio's animators brought the company back to where Walt had begun so long ago. *Beauty and the Beast* even broke out of the animation award ghetto to land an Oscar nomination for Best Picture at a time when there were only five nominations in this category.

However, there were occasional missteps. *Pocahontas* is bland, and its storyline is a bit flat. Ariel of *The Little Mermaid*, like Snow White, Sleeping Beauty, and Cinderella, makes the decision to get married to a man she barely knows and give up her voice. The studio did not always hit it out of the ballpark, but the new direction and new quality were a most welcome change. Audiences were once again pleased to invite one of the nation's most famous companies into their lives.

Pixar and Computer Animation

American animation history does not rest on Disney alone. While Disney is undeniably the foundation of the full development of the industry, there have always been other American competitors. Each historical period has seen the rise of other creative takes. Each period has also seen the rise of technological changes that have brought an essential transformation to the industry. In recent decades, technological progress and imaginative storytelling have continued to go hand in hand. Just as methods like rotoscoping and the creation of hand-painted cels made it possible to create full-length animation features much more easily and quickly, so too has the rise of computing power in the modern world. The increase in computing power has played an integral role in the ability of animated studios to craft new features on tight schedules. New technology has also created the ability to make new movies at lower cost while still meeting the highest possible quality standards.

One animation company saw the power of computer animation and ran with it. Pixar has much in common with the start of Disney Studios. Like Disney, Pixar has broken through boundaries and shown what is possible in animation. In a sense, the studio began like Walt Disney in seizing the moment. Like Disney's embrace of new technology such as Technicolor and television, Pixar staffers found computer animation an incredible opportunity. Here, they found an outlet for the creative process as Disney Studios had done with *Snow White*. Unlike Disney in the mid-1930s, however, the studio was well funded from the very first.

Pixar began in 1979 as part of Lucasfilm's computer division. The company's goal was to create new forms of technology that could be directly applied to the film industry. As Disney had done, Lucasfilm attracted incredible talent from all over the globe. By the mid-1980s, the potential possibilities in the use of computer animation were already apparent to computer scientists like Ed Catmull. It was left to some of the most innovative minds since Disney to develop them. In 1985, the division was sold to Steve Jobs. Initially, Jobs wanted to sell computers that were capable of producing high-quality imagery. With a price tag of over $100,000 per computer, however, only about 100 were sold. Financial partnership with Disney was where the company found true success and totally revolutionized the entire industry. Their Computer Animation System (CAPS) meant that studios no longer had to resort to hand-drawn cels that took so long to create. Disney officials fully embraced the new system, as it allowed for both quality and a fast turnaround.

Getting rid of the need for cels meant that animation was easier and less costly to produce. Company officials at Pixar also embarked on animation efforts of their own. John Lasseter, later forced out of the company after a series of sexual harassment allegations, was one of the chief creative minds behind this process. Short films like *Luxo Jr.* in 1986 and *Tin Toy* in 1988 earned Academy Award nominations and critical acclaim. Still, animation remained expensive as it had when Disney was striving for quality. The company's expenses were met by Steve Jobs, who contributed a massive cash infusion over the next several years. In 1995, Pixar released the full-length feature *Toy Story*. Just as *Snow White* had taken the industry and audiences in an unexpected and delighted place, the same would prove true of *Toy Story*. As the world's first "entirely computer-animated feature film," it was a technological triumph. Not only that, but *Toy Story* was a huge financial and critical success. Disney was part of Pixar early on. Officials at Disney offered Pixar a deal: they would help finance and distribute the company's first three films for 12.5 percent of the box office.

Over the next decade, Pixar continued to explore the possibilities in computer-generated animation with films that were both commercial and incredible artistic successes. From *Monsters, Inc.* to *Finding Nemo*, Pixar was at the center of a new Golden Age of Animation. In 2006, Disney went from providing some financing to the company to buying it outright. CEO Bob Iger paid more than $7.4 billion for Pixar. The hits would continue with works like *WALL-E* and *Up*. Under Disney's leadership, the result has been an animation juggernaut that has made the Pixar brand synonymous with quality animation.

As ever, critics question whether it is possible for Pixar to retain the creative fire that drove their early efforts. Ed Catmull, who pushed the company and the industry in new directions as a computer scientist, argued that the studio needed new movies rather than sequels. Since Disney has taken over the company, however, it has continued to churn out sequels that often fail to live up the company's blazing initial creative vision. At the same time, it is equally likely to see the kind of innovation that Disney officials believe so necessary to continue to advance Walt Disney's creative ideals.

Moving Forward

At every turn, Disney as a company has benefited in part because it has been shaped by a handful of strong personalities. Two men, Walt and Roy

Disney, took the idea of Disney and made it a going concern from little more than a handful of drawings. After they died, the Disney brothers were succeeded by a succession of leaders who have had an impact for better, and occasionally for worse. While no one has the same fundamental impact on the very formation of Disney that Walt did, it is undeniable that the people at the top have taken charge and forced changes both large and small. CEOs like Michael Eisner offered as distinct a vision for Disney as Walt and Roy did. After Roy died, Donn Tatum and E. Card Walker led the company for the next 10 years, a period when the company essentially remained in stasis. Efforts focused on making relatively minor movies that were not that popular with the public, as well as developing Disneyland and Disney World even further.

The position and prominence of Disney CEO came into a further national spotlight in the 1980s. Ronald W. Miller was the husband of Disney's oldest daughter, Diane. His father-in-law brought him into the company in varied roles, including producer and director. He also was the company's CEO for four years. During this time, Miller was instrumental in establishing the Disney Channel and creating an outlet for movies aimed at adults via Disney's Touchstone division. At the same time, he faced a fierce attack from Wall Street. The financial industry saw the company and its assets as unvalued and undercapitalized. Miller attempted to fend off a hostile takeover from corporate raiders. With tactics such as poison pills and an expensive stock buyback, they succeeded in dividing the management of the company. These were hugely disliked by the company's insiders, and the board of directors, and Miller made enemies of many equally powerful Disney insiders.

Within a year, Miller was ousted by Eisner, Paramount president and Disney CEO. Eisner took charge of Disney from 1984 to 2005. As head of Disney, Walt Disney usually paid little attention to finances. Profits tended to be plowed right back into the company for the next venture that he had in mind. The company went public in 1957 with an initial public offering (IPO) that was largely successful. As the end of his career approached and the company went public, Disney seized his moment for vast personal profit. He created a private company intended to keep access to certain funds for his family alone. It would eventually be known as Retlaw Enterprises. The private company played an integral and largely hidden part in the company's operations, occasionally to the disadvantage of shareholders. From 1955 to 1981, Retlaw Enterprises earned $75 million, which was to become his family's private fortune. Profitable contracts that might have been shared with shareholders were sometimes diverted to Retlaw instead. Shareholders began to play an increasingly important role in how the company was run as the company matured. These investors also did remarkably well with the Disney IPO, with a massive increase in value over the coming years. At the same time, officials running the company's board felt that still more could be done to increase the company's output, shore up its reputation, and deliver more value for them.

The corporate raiders were not welcomed by the company's leaders. Despite anger at the reaction in the financial sector, such challenges ultimately played a crucial role in pushing the company to make much-needed changes. They would lead to a renewed sense of inventive energy. The coming years after the battles with Wall Street saw the kind of hard choices that Walt Disney had faced: the push between creativity and the need to deliver financial value. Under Eisner's leadership, Disney stock prices rose to new heights. Highly lauded new movies hit the screen. He expanded the company in new and often incredibly profitable directions. Seven new Disney parks came into being under his tenure.

The company expanded into television networks, stage plays, and even sports teams. ABC had given Walt Disney the funds to start Disneyland and the ability to reach a huge segment of the American public. Eisner bought the network. He even took over Walt Disney's role as host of *The Wonderful World of Disney* TV show in 1986.

Amid some amazing triumphs, Eisner's work as CEO was also marked by labor disputes and corporate infighting. His personal compensation also frequently sparked tremendous outrage. In 1993, the company's profits fell 63 percent, to $299.8 million. That same year, Eisner made $203.1 million. He was not only the nation's highest-paid CEO of a publicly held company, but he also took a full 68 percent of the company's total profits. Revenues would later soar into the billions under his supervision, even as his compensation continued to rise. In a review of his ultimate impact, the *New York Times* summed up his work at Disney thus: "Under Mr. Eisner's tenure, Disney grew from a small theme-park operator and movie studio into a sprawling media company." In 2005, Eisner was ousted in a campaign led once again by stockholders and members of the board of directors.

Over the next 15 years, Eisner was followed by Robert Iger, and then Robert Chapek. Iger spent his entire career in the entertainment field. Under his supervision, labor relations efforts were improved, to the benefit of the company and their employees. Disney saw new movie studio acquisitions, including Marvel Entertainment, Lucasfilm, and the outright purchase of Pixar. Theme parks at home and abroad were expanded in new directions that brought in revenue and acclaim.

In the aftermath of Walt Disney's death, the company was on essentially firm financial ground. At the same time, this era also saw Disney pull back from what had been a premier role in the creation of the global animation industry. Over the next 20 years, Disney had fans but was no longer regarded as the chief voice of the industry. When a much-needed revamp came along, the result was a stronger and more vibrant company, again at the heart of the American entertainment industry. Company leadership, although often brash and occasionally greedy, brought some of the same sense of risk taking and a willingness to experiment that had marked Disney's creative and fiscal sensibilities. When Walt Disney died, the potential for even greater reward was there for the taking. Decades later, the company is as he had left it in many ways. Theme parks attract massive crowds throughout the year. Movies, both animated and live action, rake in huge profits. "Disney" continues to be shorthand for the remarkable global influence of the American entertainment industry.

CHAPTER THREE

Disneyland, Disney World, and the Creation of Southern California and Florida in the Public Mind

Mickey Mouse, Donald Duck, Pluto, and Goofy are original Disney creations. After the Golden Age of Animation and the end of World War II, Disney Studios hummed along. For Walt Disney, this period was marked by a soft landing and a desire to sit back and retreat from the world. It didn't last very long. His restless mind began to think again about a new project that would attract fans and keep the Disney name front and center. In retrospect, the work that Disney Studios did during the Golden Age fits nicely into the world of American art. The studio's creations expressed a unique American take on a worldwide art form. At the time of their original release, Disney's films endured criticism ranging from tepid to openly contemptuous. Many of these early films would later be regarded with the sort of reverence that people tend to reserve for viewing copies of the Declaration of Independence in the National Archives.

From the 1930s until the opening of Disneyland, the studio was always on the literal verge of insolvency. Animation of any kind, especially of the sort of lavish production seen in *Sleeping Beauty*, with intense details that took years to bring to life, was expensive and would remain so during Walt's life. Good animation also took a great deal of time. *Sleeping Beauty* required over five years to fine-tune to his personal satisfaction. Animation was where the studio's original fame lay. Even as Walt Disney supervised many new pictures, however, another idea began to take hold of his life: a theme park.

Theme parks have a long history. In the medieval period, fairs were held on a periodic basis. Participants had a chance to get together in the town center and shop for both local goods and items from other parts of the globe. As people gathered, they could watch demonstrations of traveling groups of performers and see exotic animals brought from afar. Many such fairs did not take place during a set period or time. The concept of public gardens where people could get together in public began to take shape in Europe during the early modern period. Starting during the 18th century, Londoners could enjoy the delights of Vauxhall Gardens. Here, for the price of a single shilling, they could get away from the urban crowds to walk through acres of well-tended gardens, admire paintings, watch fireworks displays, and listen to live music. Spectacles like the re-creation of Napoleon's defeat at Waterloo attracted huge crowds. In 1843, Copenhagen's famed Tivoli Gardens was another immediate hit. The gardens began as a simple park and later evolved into a modern amusement park. Today, they remain one of the city's most visited attractions.

Americans were just as happy as their European counterparts to have fun exploring new outdoor novelties. Early American amusement parks were places where people could have a picnic and enjoy some time with their families on their rare days off. In the latter half of the 19th century, this all began to change. The 1893 World's Columbian Exposition in Chicago proved to be an unlikely spur for the creation of the contemporary forerunner to the contemporary amusement park. World fairs had been held many times before, but the one in Chicago differed in that it separated the amusements from the area containing halls devoted to showing off exhibitions of manufactured items. Chicago's fair attracted the attention of entrepreneur George C. Tilyou. He returned home to Brooklyn with the kind of inspiration and determination that Disney understood so well. His permanent version of the temporary amusements he saw in Chicago became Steeplechase Park, which opened in 1897 in Coney Island, New York City. Along with the adjacent Luna Park and Dreamland, Steeplechase Park became the place to be during the summer for many lower-income New Yorkers. Located at the tip of the borough, with a beach next to the Atlantic Ocean, Coney Island was an easy day trip for millions of people.

Coney Island, like Disneyland, brought in travelers from all around the world eager to see cutting-age American culture and technology. Here, they could enjoy a vast array of pleasures that combined ideas taken from other places and a startling, bold originality that would reshape the very concept of American leisure time. People could race against each other on mechanical horses and ride live elephants. Firefighters put out fires on the half hour. Science and technology were also there, in the form of exhibitions like early incubators designed to care for premature babies. The parks prefigured later attractions at Epcot with attractions that offered Americans a glimpse at the world beyond their shores. Gondolas took them on canals designed to call Venice to mind, while an entire copy of a Japanese teahouse provided time in the shade and a cup of something familiar and warm. Poor management, a devastating 1911 fire, and the Great Depression eventually brought attendance down. The parks became a mere whisper in the public mind. Coney Island was at best an obscurity, largely confined to visits by New Yorkers in a neighborhood dominated by public housing. Places like Dreamland gradually faded into the background away from national attention. The words "Coney Island" became synonymous with the idea of a public space where people could have unexpected and irreverent good times. Walt Disney took that concept and reinvented it.

Los Angeles Before Disneyland

The Disney brothers found Los Angeles a congenial place. Like Kansas City, it had a sense of energy and a feeling that things were going to happen at any time. The two fit right in. Eventually, the brothers not only made this city their home base, but they also played a small yet undeniably significant role in how the world views Los Angeles. Los Angeles was not an easy fit for the kind of theme park Disney wanted. The city was too full of people in search of a dream, who often left their families behind in the process. National papers were full of the comings and goings of Hollywood film stars, who seemed to have a sense of morals that didn't quite suit the kind of small-town America Disney loved so much.

Walt would tap into the Los Angeles that was coming into being as the 1950s unfolded and postwar conformity became the desired ideal. The idea of Disneyland would ultimately take a sleepy corner of the city and make it an icon of the desirable American family vacation. Just as those aspiring to a career in the movie industry came to Los Angeles, parents looking for what they perceived as the perfect place to spend time with their families came to Anaheim. For a few hours, adults and their children could immerse themselves in Disney's fantasy worlds. A vacation at Disneyland was to be—and still is—as American to the world as a trip to the Grand Canyon or a tour of the White House.

For Los Angelenos, Disneyland started as a bit of a surprise. Despite relatively tight control of the media by Disney and his company, it was clear that something was up on the outskirts of their city. When it opened, people lined up the previous night just for a chance to enter the place that Walt Disney talked about on television. Over the next decades, Disneyland became as famous in Los Angeles as the Hollywood sign and the Dolby Theater, where the Oscars were given out. Locals understandably grumble about issues such as unwanted traffic, but the park is just as much a favorite destination for them as it is for people all over the globe.

The history of Disneyland, like the history of Los Angeles, is one of golden expectations from the first, but it had a rocky start. Conflicts between the park and the region's residents created tension (and still do today). Walt's park would ultimately serve as a blueprint for the modern amusement park and prove what could be done with a few acres of land near a thriving community. Disneyland would also serve to illustrate the process where Disney was fond of erasing a rough and complicated history in favor of a more syrupy patina. In his park, everything is always immaculate, and people can burst into song at any moment. For so many, Disneyland continues to offer the quintessential sun-drenched California playground.

El Pueblo de Nuestra Señora la Reina de los Ángeles del Río Porciúncula, or "the town of our lady the Queen of Angels of the River Porciúncula," has been inhabited for thousands of years. America's second-largest city was originally home to a varied group of small bands of indigenous hunter-gatherer tribes until Europeans decided to travel to the edge of the American continent. In the 1700s, Spanish colonizers made their way west, and in 1781, 44 of them officially established El Pueblo. The outpost was intended to be a small farming village on the banks of the Porciúncula River. A handful of settlers were quickly followed by even more people from Europe, who were happy to establish a new community in the very far reaches of the New World.

Spanish control of the area was overthrown when Mexico gained independence in 1821. Settlement remained relatively sparse in the coming years. The first census, in 1841, showed that the area had a total population of 141. In 1847, after a brief battle, the United States took control of the area. Two years later, the region underwent enormous transformation. Gold was discovered in Sacramento. A convenient community was needed to provide things and services for the miners. By 1881, the city was officially connected with the rest of the United States when the Southern Pacific Railroad laid track that linked to Los Angeles directly.

Over the next 30 years, Los Angeles continued to be a sleepy little town known largely as a place with abundant light and the ready availability of fresh citrus fruit. The city that the world knows as a place of dreams on the large screen began to take shape when the director D. W. Griffith found that the sunshine and access to low-wage workers made it an ideal spot for filming. Other movie industry officials followed his lead. Los Angeles rapidly became a hotbed of movie activity, taking the crown from New York City with ease. Hollywood, previously no more than a dot on the map, was in the center of it all.

When Americans thought of Los Angeles, they thought of glamorous people doing glamorous things. People flocked here to escape the dull gray winter in search of something that they could not always quite define. For many, it was the golden city that allowed them to shake off the shackles of their previous lives and make themselves new again. Los Angeles embodied that fundamentally most American idea that second acts were possible. The city saw massive numbers of people flock to it from the rest of the country. Los Angeles was their chosen destination. It would become the population center of the West Coast. In doing so, the newcomers started the long climb to turn the city into the second-most-populous city in the country. Philadelphia and Baltimore felt leaden and shackled by convention, while Los Angeles hummed like a brand-new electric light bulb. By 1924, more than a million people had made it their home.

Like others before him, Walt Disney saw Los Angeles as a chance to fulfill his most important dreams. After his studio in Kansas City failed, he purchased a train ticket and made Los Angeles his own chance for a do-over. For Disney, Los Angeles would remain his home base and the place he loved most, even as he extolled the virtues of the American small town. His work often took him to other parts of the world, but Los Angeles was where he raised his daughters, built a house, and started a business that remade the field of American animation.

He chose Los Angeles as the place for the kind of amusement park he had in mind for many reasons. Snowy Brooklyn meant the amusement parks in Coney Island at the foot of the borough were closed a good portion of the year. The areas around Los Angeles also offered another relative advantage: cheaper land. As World War II drew to a close, Disney was staying closer and closer to home. The park he wanted was going to open right outside his door.

A New American Theme Park

Elias Disney, Walt's father, was a carpenter for the 1893 World's Fair. His son Walt often heard him talk about his contributions to the fair that brought Chicago to national and international attention. When the family moved to Kansas City, Electric Park was waiting for them. Electric Park was the local Kansas City amusement park. It was typical of the period, with many kinds of rides. Visitors found a large pool for cooling off during the humid Kansas summers and games of chance masquerading as games of skill. The park was an outgrowth of the need for trolleys to keep up their ridership on weekends.

These attractions were hugely popular with the public, but they were often regarded with deep suspicion by a certain segment of the community. Little attention was paid to safety. People were encouraged to take physical risks on slides and coasters that had an air of daring that few could find anywhere else. That was part of the charm for many visitors, but it didn't make the park any more attractive for cautious parents. Electric Park had to shut down its famous Circle Swing after an accident injured eight people. Alcohol was part of the fun, and an indulgence that adults adored even in the middle of Prohibition. Beer was served in large amounts by a brewery right next door until it was finally shut down in 1925. Advertised as "the Coney Island of Kansas City," the park formed a visual memory that Disney tapped into when thinking about the kind of park he wanted to call his own. For the rest of his life, he would remember the way it felt as a kid to enter fantasyland. He would also remember the train that circled it and the fireworks marking the end of the day. Those were two elements that he would make part of his Disneyland.

Disney wanted to update the concept of the modern family that he knew as a young man. His park would be cleaner, less disreputable, and far more about centering family life rather than cheap thrills. He hoped it would shake off the tawdry and tattered ghosts of Coney Island that clung like mud to the very idea of amusement parks. By the late 1940s, Disney had a model nearby. Knott's Berry Farm is a Los Angeles–based amusement park. Begun as an outgrowth of a restaurant that served the farm's beloved berry pies, it would later grow into something far more. Founded in the 1920s, the park was as much about attractions as it was about dining and pies. At that time, there were a series of fun places to enjoy, such as rock gardens and waterfalls where visitors could cool off while they waited for a table. There was also a ghost town and many shops. Walt Disney was fascinated by the park's ability to draw in visitors willing to wait to see a few attractions and enjoy a chicken dinner. Over the next decade, the park's owners and Disney became friends and admirers. Walter Knott and his wife were honored guests when Disneyland opened. He would follow in Disneyland's footsteps, draw on Disneyland's traffic, and become a classic American amusement park, with lots of rides and its eponymous homemade pies.

By 1952, Disney was ready to start talking about his plans. He gave an interview to the *Burbank Daily Review* in which he let the public in on his plans. The park he had in mind would be a modest endeavor; he said, "Disneyland will be something of a fair, a playground, a community center, a museum of living facts and a showplace of beauty and magic." He implied that the park was a small-scale, community-based venture in which finances were at best a minor consideration and any attractions would be secondary to a simple stroll in the park. This sounded good, but it was a lie.

Plunging full steam ahead, Disney hired help and let them in on his larger ambitions. Their goal was to find "about 150 acres somewhere in Southern California." By then, Disney had started to fully flesh out the ideas that he had had in mind for his park for the past few years. His own paradise would begin with a Main Street based on his early years in a small town in Missouri. Once inside, there would be four separate lands for visitors to explore on foot. Adventureland, Fantasyland, Frontierland, and the World of Tomorrow all represented different facets of the United States as he saw them.

His ideas for an amusement park would also be different in other ways. Traditional parks could be seen looming in the distance long before people got there. That was part of the way they were advertised. People saw large rides before they entered the park. This was all far too showy for a man determined to keep a sense of mystery for his visitors. Disneyland would lie behind a landscaped berm so that all was not visible until the guests were actually inside. The ideal was a self-contained area akin to the movie theater, where nothing would interfere with the world of fantasy and fun Disney wanted. The park would also be nowhere near any body of water. Walt Disney did not want sand on his rides or bathers with wet towels on his streets. He did not want little children wearing bathing suits down Main Street and slopping water all over the place for the workers to clean up. He wanted an experience that he could control completely in the same way he'd controlled the names of the dwarfs of *Snow White* and the colors of *Dumbo*.

Anaheim, the eventual location for Disneyland, was settled in the 1850s. By the end of that decade, it was the center of the small but growing American wine industry. When a bacterium caused the wine grapes to wither on the vine, locals sought another product option. They found it in oranges. Thanks to refrigerated cars, oranges went from an exotic delicacy mentioned by Laura Ingalls Wilder as a special Christmas treat to something that the average person might consume once a week. When Disney's firm found Anaheim, the town had much to recommend it as the site of a park. Because it was miles from the California coast, it enjoyed an inland climate, with warm weather nearly all year long. Land here was relatively cheap compared to other parts of the state.

Disney wanted the whole thing to be a secret until he was ready for an official announcement and the massive publicity that he knew would follow. To that end, he had a firm put out misinformation that his efforts were focused on the San Fernando Valley. The total cost for the land was $879,000. There were two real questions. The first was exactly how to get what he wanted from some orange groves and a handful of trailers. The second was how to get more funding, as it rapidly became apparent that he didn't have even a fraction of the money he really needed.

The latter was a lot easier than it might have seemed to outsiders. Disney spent much of his career managing to convince people to follow his plans, both emotionally and financially, even when they seemed nearly impossible. When work began on *Snow White*, Walt spent hours acting out scenes for his animators. They had the chance to participate in his vision firsthand. The same was true of his plans for the new amusement park. In many significant ways, the amusement park was an even harder sell than *Snow White*. Investors and his employees knew all about movies. Disney had a long prior track record getting animation on screen and pleasing audiences all over the world. The new park he had in mind had no such antecedents. Amusement parks were not a national priority, nor were they particularly prestigious.

This endeavor was not likely to add to his many industry kudos. A park with rides was not the kind of place that investors initially thought might burnish the Disney name. His workers and their unions were enthusiastic about his ideas but not entirely convinced it could be done when Disney wanted it done. Investors felt that the emphasis on cleanliness and the use of landscaping were details that the general public would neither notice nor care about. Plans for rides based on movies seemed equally impossible and unrealistic. Others worried that this was little more than a grandiose vanity project, destined to suck up money and fail spectacularly.

Certain aspects of the park simply weren't going to work as planned initially. Over time, they became bogged down in details that made it all rough going. The jungle for the proposed Jungle Cruise ride required importing live materials from places as far away as Africa and Brazil. Maintaining it also required a great deal of attention from the park's gardeners once opened. Walt Disney was not pleased by the existing rides he saw on the market. They felt cluttered, downscale, gaudy, and dark. His plans for a shiny new future needed something different. He and his team would come up with ideas for rides and other attractions that aimed at an optimistic view instead of one fraught with a hint of sexual tension. Unlike Coney Island and Electric Park, Disney would allow no alcohol consumption. There would be no beer or wine at this park for most of the public for many years. Only select members of Club 33, a Disney members-only restaurant, were permitted to drink on the grounds. The anti-alcohol policy at Disneyland remained in place until spring 2019, when alcohol was allowed at the *Star Wars* section of the park. Other parks, including Disney World and Epcot, have provided for consumption of alcoholic beverages under certain circumstances. Rides at his park ranged from the standard (a carousel with parts ironically salvaged in part from one at the Coney Island that Disney disdained) to the teacup spin that took inspiration from Disney's *Alice in Wonderland*.

Disneyland began to take shape under Walt Disney's highly detailed direction. When not directing the park, he was extremely busy finding the financing for it. ABC officials were bewildered at best. They were not entirely pleased at the prospect of tying their brand to an unproven and even possibly sleazy concept. But ABC officials also wanted a known name and famous voice to give their network an identity. They were willing to overlook such future issues if it meant giving their network a boost in the public eye today.

On October 27, 1954, Disney came to the small screen. His first program, called *The Disneyland Story*, was entirely given over to Disneyland as he saw it. It was an act of daring to bring an entire hour devoted to a concept that was not even ready for the public. Americans took immediate notice, with a huge 52 percent share of the viewing audience that night. That was the first time the American public heard about plans for Disneyland. It was the first of many such television programs Disney devoted to his amusement park.

He needed the money and the American public on his side. The park was proving to be an endless money sink. Disney thought that he might need about $1.5 million to get it going. By the time the program aired, that money had long since been spent. Additional funds flowed in in the aftermath of the *Davy Crockett* miniseries. Not only was that series a huge hit, but it also brought millions into the studio's coffers in the form of sales of coonskin caps. Disney had already spent $11 million on Disneyland. Even with all the money he showered on the space, it was still nowhere near ready for a single guest. By publicizing his efforts, Disney also was setting up a timeline. The park had to be open to the public by the date he'd set up or else he'd risk disappointing millions of viewers and ruining his reputation.

To raise even more money, he and his team turned to large corporations and sponsorships. Just as ABC had been thrilled to have an alliance with Disney, many leading American companies were equally happy to be part of his next ideas, even if they weren't quite sure where he was going with them. Main Street would present the introduction to the rest of the space. Here was a chance to show off familiar American brands and offer something that people instantly understood. Visitors could grab a cup of coffee at the Maxwell House Coffee Shop, enjoy a cold drink at the Coca-Cola Refreshment Center, and have a scoop of ice cream at the Carnation Ice Cream Parlor.

Many companies took the turn-of-the-century theme Disney wanted quite seriously. For instance, Upjohn Pharmaceuticals aimed for total realism. When the park opened, two licensed pharmacists took orders behind the counter. Hundreds of objects pertaining to the work of pharmaceutical companies five decades ago lined the walls. Each had been scoured from places like attics and basements all over the nation. Other parts of the park also had obvious corporate advertising too. Visitors could stop off for lunch at the Casa de Fritos Mexican Cantina. Two tuna companies, StarKist and Chicken of the Sea, even bickered about their right to be part of the action. As Chicken of the Sea had been approached first, it won the day. Even Ray A. Kroc, the man who was about to expand McDonalds from a tiny chain into a household name and entirely transform the fast food industry, offered to be part of the effort, but it never quite jelled. He would open up his first fast food outlet a mere three months before Disneyland had its first guest. Lots of American companies wanted to tie their names to Disney. Their faith and contributions helped bring the project to life and enabled Disney to show how many sources of revenue he could find even before the park opened to the public.

Contracts at Disneyland did not come cheap. Rent was $20 a square foot along Main Street and a nearly equally hefty $15 in other areas. Main Street was home to some of the nation's best-known companies. They were not the only places the company lobbied for business. Locals found space that helped tie the park to the surrounding area. The Hollywood-Maxwell Brassiere Company, slightly at odds with the wholesale image the company sought to convey, nevertheless had a store devoted to intimate apparel, with an exhibit on the history of the bra. Well-known names jumped in, looking for chances to sell to customers in other parts of the park. Kodak agreed to pay $28,000 a year for five years, while Trans World Airlines agreed to its own $45,000 contract.

Disney needed the money. The teacups ride alone cost over $100,000. Little details that he insisted on, like the landscaping, were also eating up money. He wanted all the lands in Disneyland to be unique and feel different as visitors strolled from one place to the next. That meant a steady stream of cash as the work continued. What was once a mind-blowing sum in raised capital was obviously going to cost $15 million—or perhaps even more. Disney took out loans from every source. He even cashed out his life insurance policy. His wife, Lillian, was terrified that their family would be left with no assets to live on should the park fail. Workers worked massive amounts of overtime, running up labor costs even higher just to meet his looming deadline. Unions like the Teamsters argued over who would get contracts from the company, while the Orange County plumbers and asphalt layers even went on strike for a brief time.

As his park continued to shape up, each area had a specific plan and character. Main Street was an homage to his roots and the idealized childhoods that he hoped the rest of the country might share. Frontierland harked back even further in time, when his own family was still in Canada. Adventureland was about bringing characters from Disney movies to life for fans. Only one area lacked a firm definition. Tomorrowland remained on the back burner during much of the planning process. Disney even thought of scrapping it entirely, or at least delaying that part until the park was already open. He wasn't exactly sure what he might offer the public.

After much thought, cars took center stage. Autopia, where people can drive around a track, was the primary attraction in Tomorrowland and the most enduring as well. Tomorrowland underwent radical revision multiple times, but it remained a lasting symbol of the kind of optimism Disney hoped to embody, along with a sense that there would always be something new for people to discover. Here, he previewed the American interstate highway system that would come about just a short time later under President Dwight D. Eisenhower. After Main Street, Disney officials wanted visitors to have a continued sense of wonder as they walked around the park. The goal was to bring them to each land by encouraging further exploration of areas of interest just a few feet away. Disney wanted people to spend all day walking from one section to the next and feeling enraptured with the whole process of exploration.

Right in front of Main Street, one of the most famous attractions of all time gradually came to life. Sleeping Beauty Castle, like so many other attractions he had in mind, was modeled on an ideal form. In a sense, it is the idea of a castle instead of the real thing. Much to the complete dismay of budget-watcher Roy Disney, while most of the parts of the castle are fiberglass, the gold on top of the spires is real. Given the sturdiness of the material in the warm California sun, it was actually cost effective over the long term.

Frontierland had rides with real animals that children could pet, a Disney detail that he knew would please parents and kids alike. He'd wanted to bring in actual elephants and other wild animals, but he had to reconsider on the grounds that they would add cost and provide little in the way of entertainment. The tallest structure in Disneyland was actually the Moonliner. This was a Trans World Airlines–sponsored exhibit intended to show what a ride to the Moon might look like in the (then) far-off 1980s. The exhibit was taken down a few years later, but parts of it could be seen standing in a corner until the 1980s.

These were among the handful of objects that could be seen from outside the park, along with the train. Disney wanted a park that would lure guests and keep them intrigued once inside. While the Moonliner wasn't an especially accurate depictions of real-life objects, there were plenty of details at every turn that were all about intense authenticity. The Mark Twain Steamboat aimed at an intricate, accurate depiction, and got there under Disney's close supervision. It's a 5/8-scale boat specially designed for him. The boat, known as a "stern-wheeler," was the first functional boat of its type built in the country for over five decades. Research to create the boat, dig the river where it would take passengers, and fill that river was another project that added layers of yet more money to the funds he needed to get to opening day.

Despite all the intense rush, the park still continued to have a great many open areas with little else besides some greenery and a place to sit. In addition, Disney also faced a deadline that could not be missed. Everything had to be there ready and waiting by July 17, the agreed-upon deadline with Disney's partnership with ABC. Disney made plans to broadcast a 90-minute introduction on that day on television to millions of people all over the United States. Advertising spots were sold out by March. Disney had backed himself into a corner that left him with few options but to keep going.

It was a familiar place for him. Getting a project like Disneyland up and running, on budget and ready for the critics, while somehow avoiding bankruptcy, was the kind of act that had defined his career from the very first. The park was where he put all that he had learned in place over the course of his 25 years in show business. Like his movies, it required intense imagination, attention to every single possible detail, revamping of an already-existing form familiar to many people, and a willingness to envision the future and his company's place inside it. His park also required the ability to pull back when it was clear that some parts were simply not going to work out. Rides were rethought as needed and space left for future expansion.

Just like the studio's movies, Disneyland needed deep pockets and a sense of innate showmanship that could capture public attention and keep it there for long periods of time. The former, Disney had managed to scrounge; the latter meant putting himself out there for the public more than ever. All the efforts of his team proved to be enough—but just barely. When the park officially opened, huge crowds gathered to see what was about to happen. The crowd swelled to an even bigger size, as scalpers sold counterfeit tickets and others climbed the fences even as officials tried to get them to stop. The massive numbers were useful in showing what Disney had to do to fix the park's issues in the months ahead.

Opening day at Disneyland was rather like the first day of school. Visitors to a strange new place they'd never seen before were full of excitement. They shared a sense that something big was about to happen. Their expectations were not quite met, despite tremendous preparation, an obvious general plan, and the hint that something bigger was in progress but had not yet taken shape yet. Lines to enter stretched as far as the eye could see well before the official opening. The throngs were not well managed, to the dismay of the poor visitors stuck with inadequate bathroom access. Dead grass was spray-painted green because there was no more money for landscaping, and the asphalt was so soft that visitors lost their shoes in it and had to pull them out full of pitted gravel. Charming touches like the medieval rocks and other decor details in Fantasyland had to be put in later, while the rides were housed in what were essentially large boxes. He and his crew had stayed up the night before frantically trying to get all the work done. They knew the plans for the place weren't there and wouldn't be there for at least some time. The total costs for the entire park at that point soared beyond an astounding $17 million.

The initial reviews were dreadful. A columnist wrote, "To sum up, Disneyland was a disappointment." Others were equally critical. Headlines told of huge crowds of unhappy people and an expensive experience that was hardly worth it. The local freeway wasn't finished. Traffic in and out of the park was almost terrifying as drivers tried to figure out where parking began and how to get to the park gates. Dave MacPherson had the honor of being the first guest who wasn't a Disney family member and got a lifetime pass to show for it. He was quickly followed by more than 6,000 people just waiting to get in. By the end of the day, over 25,000 others had followed him.

Not only was the park not entirely finished, but it also cost a lot of money to take part in the activities. Previous amusement parks had been largely about letting crowds in for a small sum and then charging them for lots of extras. Disney knew that he had to earn the money to keep the park running and pay his employees, as well as his plans for expansion. So he charged a fee to park, and then more money for admission to the actual park, and then even more money for rides and food. A family could easily spend a significant sum when the rides, snacks, and all other extras were tallied up. The park had been so rushed that managers were forced to choose between bathrooms and water fountains. Choosing bathrooms meant guests were walking around in the hot sun and paying to buy drinks to stave off dehydration. A gas leak led to flames at the foot of Sleeping Beauty Castle, while the Mark Twain Riverboat nearly sank from too many passengers. Ronald Reagan never appeared in any Disney films, but he did play a starring role in the opening of the park. Reagan was the host of a special devoted to the opening of the park. However, things were so disorganized that even he had to scale a fence to enter the park and show everyone what it looked like.

The press gradually warmed up to the new park over the next several days and weeks, in part because Disney was very good at working with the media. He'd endured bad reviews before and come out on top. Share prices dropped precipitously, but Disney was still Disney, with all the magic that the name had come to imply in the public mind for nearly two decades. People wanted to see what the company had done. Even in the middle of a heat wave the following August, they kept coming to Disneyland. By the time January rolled around, rough projections for the number of visitors had been vastly exceeded. In 1956, 4 million people visited Disneyland.

Within a year, many of the initial obstacles had been worked out. Even if critics weren't entirely pleased with what Hollywood had called "Walt's Folly," the public sure was. Surveys showed over 93 percent of visitors were happy with the experience and felt that it was worth the money. Within two months, a million people had seen Disneyland in person. Within a year, more than 3 million people flocked to Anaheim, bringing their money with them. By the end of the park's first full year of operation, total corporate revenues for the entire company were $24 million. At long last, Disneyland and the company as a whole were totally in the black for the foreseeable future. Later developments, such as the ability to pay a single price for admission and a set total number of rides, would make the park more affordable for many families.

All the months of striving and pushing paid off. Disneyland was one of Walt Disney's final projects, and perhaps his most enduring and financially successful one. Unlike his movies, Disneyland allowed him to make an endless series of revisions. This satisfied his innate desire to tinker with his projects over and over. Once it was a going concern, he would come back and make changes. He would also spend the rest of his life just walking around the place and taking it all in with great delight as fans shyly asked for his autograph. The man from the middle of nowhere with the harsh childhood had once again mastered a new medium and brought something original to his fellow Americans. What had been farmland was now a place of even more possibilities.

Over the next few decades, the company's tinkering led to almost constant changes in the park. Visitors were given the option of paying for a book of tickets that they could use for different rides. This was eventually abolished in favor of a single admissions fee in the 1980s. New sections such as New Orleans Square opened over the years, along with new rides like the Pirates of the Caribbean. Tomorrowland underwent massive revision and more space for roller coasters. Revisions and changes to this section continue to this day as company officials play with the notion of the meaning of tomorrow for each generation. By 1981, over 200 million people had come through the gates, making it by far the world's most visited theme park. In 2001, a second park, Disney's California Adventure, opened next door to Disneyland. Like Disneyland, the park remains unfinished—even today. The company has plenty of acres for expansion.

Walt Disney spent millions gambling on a concept that had long been relegated to some of the more shadowy corners of American life. He opened up that idea again and polished it. In the process, Disney showed that the amusement park could be about something more than adults guzzling alcohol and poorly maintained rides offering the possibility of injury with every move. As with so much of what he did in American life, he sanitized another classic American experience. Disney took away the idea of exploring the dangerous, thrilling unknown when people entered an amusement park. Under his supervision, Disneyland brought a more cloying feel to one of the more raffish, but purely enjoyable activities of the classic American summer.

In that sense, it was Walt Disney at his very worst. But the park was also him at his very best. Providing families with a place that all members could fully and safely appreciate together made Disneyland a land of memories for many Americans and their children. Little children got to meet Mickey Mouse in person, while teens took in fast roller coasters that promised and delivered delicious but safe thrills. Meanwhile, mom and dad relaxed with well-made pastries or sat on a riverboat enjoying the breezes and terrific views. He was able to bring forth a closely held, single-minded vision and forge from it the concept of a uniquely American take on an amusement park. He did this in the heart of America's most optimistic state, largely from scratch.

The park is also Disney at his most bullheaded, controlling, historically revisionist, and banal. Parts of Disneyland are arguably nothing more than hackneyed cliché and extremely long lines. Other sections offer jarring commercialized intrusions that detract from the dreamy, vaguely childlike feel that had been his ultimate aim when he first began. Despite these flaws, a visit to Disneyland is one of those quintessential American experiences that manages to symbolize the entire country in a few acres, with live shows and rides thoughtfully sheltered from the hot California sun. From rows of orange groves to detailed drawings, and then to a park ready for millions of people built in less than a year from start to finish, Disneyland also serves as an impressive monument to something larger. The park is the result of a certain kind of primal American tenacity and love of the sheer power of showmanship that was embodied in the trajectory of Walt's own life.

Finding Florida: Creating Disney World

After Disneyland became a going concern with an obviously bright future, Walt Disney made it his own personal kingdom. Once the crowds left, he'd stroll the grounds at night and then go to sleep in his own private apartment. As Disney looked around, he knew that the park was likely to take the rest of his life to bring to fruition, and even beyond that to his children's and grandchildren's lives. Unlike so many of his other ideas, this one was presented to the public warts and all.

Disney officials hoped that the park would continue to evolve. What gradually became clear to Disney and other company officials, however, was that there was plenty of room for a second site in an entirely different location. Within a short time, Disney realized that Disneyland was drawing much of its audience from California and the immediate area to the east. A mere 2 percent of all park visitors indicated that they were coming from east of the Mississippi River. Another park would likely pull people in from the second half of the country, and even more guests from Europe and other parts of the world.

Part of Walt's attention was also focused on a reimagined idea of what the perfect city could look like. He wanted to expand his pristine, idealized Main Street into other areas of American life. This concept would eventually become the Experimental Prototype Community of Tomorrow, more familiarly known as "Epcot." Just as he'd become obsessed over Disneyland, Epcot struck him with the same intensity. Epcot and the new amusement park were to become one and the same to him.

The real question was where the location of the new park would be and when it could be ready for the public. Disney officials had quite a selection. Officials all over the world knew what he'd done for Anaheim, Los Angeles, and indeed the whole of California, and they wanted him to do the same for their own communities. Walt Disney was besieged by fans all over the United States wanting a similar revenue-generating park near them. Several places captured his attention early in the process. Niagara Falls seemed a likely candidate, with a ready-made tourist base both in the United States and just over the Rainbow Bridge in Canada. New Jersey also had possibilities. An affluent suburban state and an easy commute from New York City put it at the top of the list, but it was also far from his home and would probably be open for less than half the year at best. Another Coney Island was not what he wanted. For a while, St. Louis was also a leading candidate. But all three areas had colder weather for part of the year, which was likely to eat into the park's potential operating dates.

St. Louis actually had a detailed set of plans in place before it was abandoned. Walt Disney's Riverfront Square was to be a five-story indoor affair set in the center of the American Midwest. For varied reasons, including the fact that the city was associated with alcohol consumption in the public mind and the finances weren't quite feasible, the project never got off the ground. Instead, Walt Disney found a new home. The city of Orlando and the entire state of Florida were about to undergo a massive transformation. Under the direction of the Disney brothers, they would take the city and the state from a relative backwater to one of the world's premier vacation destinations.

Like California, Florida has been inhabited for thousands of years. Historians believe that many Native American groups were living there long before Europeans showed up. These tribes had hunter-gatherer lifestyles that took full advantage of the abundant sea creatures and easy outdoor living. When Europeans came to Florida, they fought over the land at the end of the seaboard with great ferocity. Over several centuries, control of what would become Florida went back and forth between the British, Spanish, and Americans. In 1821, Florida officially became part of the United States when the European wars for control of the Americas were over. Under the direction of General Andrew Jackson, who later became president, Native Americans were brutally removed from the land and sent to the flat fields of Oklahoma. Florida became a state in 1845 and then joined the Confederacy during the Civil War. Small-scale industries such as farming were the state's primary employers.

Several inventions would remake the state into the place that the Disney brothers eventually found. The first was the railroad. American financier Henry M. Flagler made a fortune as a partner in the monopolistic Standard Oil. Flagler found the Floridian climate congenial. His investments in railroads and hotels brought people all the way to the southern tip of the state in larger numbers by the 1880s.

The second idea that made Florida before Walt Disney arrived was the creation of practical air conditioning that afforded indoor spaces for people to escape the often oppressive heat and humidity. Early efforts by Dr. John Gorrie in the 19th century gave way to the electric fan, and then to Willis Carrier and the early modern form of air conditioning. The ability to turn an occasionally harsh climate into one with readily accessible, cooler air made Florida an even more attractive destination. As personal automobiles came into fashion and became far more affordable, the railroads fell out of favor with the American public. Americans preferred their cars. Spurred by the creation of the interstate highway system and relatively inexpensive gas prices, they were taking to the road in large numbers. A trip south to the state's beaches, crystal-clear water, and constant sunshine was marketed as the ideal getaway for Americans from Chicago to New York.

Walt and Roy Disney plunged headfirst into Florida and never looked back. By 1963, Walt was engaged in wholesale efforts to buy thousands of acres. In California, he'd felt hemmed in because he soon realized he had not bought enough land before creating Disneyland. As he became more and interested in Florida, his goal was total secrecy for his new project. Orlando got a lot of Disney's attention. The central location meant that the park wouldn't be near either the gulf or the coast. Just as he'd done in Anaheim, Disney wanted a resort that would serve as a destination in itself. For him, the primary appeal of a new place was not only the opportunity to build another even larger amusement park; it was also a chance to build his ideal city—one that would house any employees and show the world how to overcome the kind of urban unrest that he and his fellow conservatives found frightening as the 1960s began to unfold. Epcot would also allow for corporate experimentation while being self-governing.

Orlando had certain things in common with Anaheim. Like Anaheim, it was located in an Orange County. Orange growing was a mainstay of the economy, along with some light manufacturing, other forms of farming, and ranching. City officials pitched their community as a climate where people could recover from serious illness or retire in the sun. However, unlike Anaheim, Orlando was not part of any larger metropolitan area. Miami, Tampa, and Atlanta, Georgia, were all a considerable drive away. There was some growth, but it was part of other projects such as Cape Canaveral, about an hour's drive away, where the gradually expanding space program occupied the lion's share of attention.

Orlando was touted as the perfect place to start a small business, as well as a hub on the way to other parts of Florida. City officials saw booms, but nothing on the order that Disney was about to bring to their community. Over the next few years, the Disney Company had a deeply complicated relationship with both the local township and the state government, which continues to the present day. In *Married to the Mouse: Walt Disney World and Orlando,* political scientist Richard Fogelsong charts what he calls a fairly "tempestuous relationship" between Disney and the region. Here, in essence, the company was able to develop a place of its own, always making it exempt from certain laws governing other Floridian companies.

By 1965, the company had spent more than $5 million to purchase over 25,000 acres. Walt and Roy Disney finally held a press conference with the blessing of Florida's governor from afar to announce their plans to the world. The finances necessary to get the park off the ground were mind-boggling. Disneyland had required $17 million and the help of a major network to get it up and running. Disney World would exceed that sum by a staggering amount.

Walt Disney died in 1966. Over the next five years, his place in the company was taken by his older brother. Roy Disney was the third of Elias Disney's sons. He was eight years older than Walt, and in a real sense Walt's third parent. He watched over his younger brother and did his best to protect him from his father's rages. The practical, calm Roy had a lot more in common with the rest of the family than Walt had. Like them, he was grounded in his time and very much in tune with what other Americans thought and felt. He was decidedly not a dreamer. He stood in firm contrast to the voluble Walt, who was so willing to take risks. In many ways, Roy was the quiet brother behind the scenes, often scrambling to find financing for his brother's projects yet again.

In his own way, in bringing Disney World to life, Roy Disney had a vast impact on a single state in a way that his brother had not quite managed with Disneyland. Roy can be credited with creating a version of modern Florida in the public eye. The establishment of Disney World transitioned the state from being simply another part of the American South to a place that pervaded the nation's and world's consciousness in much the same way California does. His work on Disney World made the state a destination not only for those seeking relief from the cold weather up north, but also for those in search of a family vacation. He would put Florida on the map for many Europeans, who found the whole notion of sunshine just as enchanting as Americans did.

Roy lacked his brother's incredible artistic vision, but he shared his fierce and ruthless persistence. In the course of the business relationship between the two brothers that began early and continued until Walt's death, the coolheaded Roy served as the anchor to his brother's impetuosity. When Walt died, many wondered if the possibility of a second Disney park died with him. Roy knew that this had been his brother's final dream, so he kept at it. The last years of Roy's life were devoted to the process of getting the new park ready for the public. Florida officials were not as favorable to the company as they had been during that first press conference, when Walt was there to speak to them directly. The new governor was a Republican. He was not entirely convinced that the state needed another Disneyland, let alone the kind of vast project the company clearly had in the mind in the heart of the state. More than twice the size of Manhattan, the land the company purchased was huge, even for a fairly undeveloped state. An impressive 481 pages of legislation went in front of state legislators, giving Disney unprecedented powers. Disney officials asked to be allowed to create their own government, with a police department, a fire department, zoning rights, and the ability to levy their own taxes and use that revenue as they pleased. Legislators balked. But they came to life again when watching Walt Disney talk about the incredible possibilities he foresaw in Epcot. That vision, more than a mere amusement park that had already been done somewhere else, caught the ear of state officials and led them to agree to Disney's terms. Even after his death, the mere sound of Walt's voice in a prerecorded video could push the Disney Company's agenda forward.

The new project differed from Disneyland in several respects. Perhaps most importantly, the timeline allowed for breathing room. Where Disneyland had been rushed into production while the nation watched each week, Disney World came to America's attention at a more meandering pace. For Roy Disney, the park served multiple purposes. The first was to serve as final memorial to his brother's legacy. In that spirit, he asked for the park to be called Walt Disney World. The second was to expand the company's brand to a new place and show that there was a market for Disney products throughout the United States.

Both goals took years to realize. Just to clear the land to start work on the park was a two-year process. The site the company purchased was mostly scrubland, with some very wet areas and native Florida plant life that had roots reaching deep into the sandy soil. Unlike Anaheim, this was a land with few connections to the rest of the country and even fewer on-site amenities. Work on the project had to be done from scratch, including constructing the roads and all the buildings. Labor was scarce in this part of the state, and strikes were common. The costs kept going up and up. What was once estimated at an astonishing $50 million soon became $100 million and finally climbed to the unreal sum of $400 million. Meanwhile, the publicity kept building. Government officials were kept apprised of the work via the corporate pipeline.

The opening date for the park was eventually set for October 1, 1971. The idea was to give workers and managers the time to get any problems worked out before the larger crowds would follow at Thanksgiving and Christmas. Company officials did not want a repeat of the problems that had plagued opening day at Disneyland. The possibility of problems with parking, disorganized and confused park employees, and those first contemptible reviews of Disneyland that had so scared stockholders and company officials were unimaginable a second time.

Like opening day at Disneyland, parts of Disney World were also left unfinished. Lack of funds combined with the rough landscape made it all hard going, even after many years of work. Disney officials also wanted room to expand. In the same way they'd done at Disneyland, several rides that would later stand out as star attractions were not ready. Just as a television show hailed the opening of Disneyland, the same was done for Disney World. The park also had themed lands that were nearly identical. There was a Main Street that called to mind Disney's childhood, yet again in idealized form. Adventureland and Bear Country were there, along with Fantasyland, Frontierland, Liberty Square, and of course the second Tomorrowland.

Roy Disney passed away three months after Disney World opened. He had been the silent partner, so often standing behind Walt and managing somehow to keep the company together financially. If Walt was the dreamer who loved nothing more than another set of visions to capture his imagination again and again, Roy was the pragmatist. Roy, for all the incredible personal business success, power, world travel, and acclaim that flowed from being the brother of Walt in Walt's own highly lauded kingdom, represented the kind of ordinariness that made him almost more of an American than the very public Uncle Walt. Unlike his younger brother, he was a man entirely of his age and background. He had a great deal in common with his eldest brother, Herbert. Offered a chance to join the Disney Company, Herbert stuck to his job as a mailman.

If Disneyland eventually blended seamlessly into the larger California landscape, Disney World had a more troublesome path to integration with Orlando and the rest of Florida. What was once a relatively small town with about 50,000 inhabitants became a worldwide destination for more than 50 million people. In the first two years alone, more than 20 million came to this part of Florida just to go to Disney World. The entire community was transformed, but not always to the benefit of locals. Some were able to sell their homes near the park at an inflated price once it became known that the Disneys wanted the place. Many others found jobs and careers in the park. Other residents found themselves rapidly priced out of housing. Once the park was opened, congestion and traffic jams extended around all areas of the city and into many parts of the region. That made commuting harder. Many jobs that Disney offered at the park were the kind of relatively low-paying service jobs that were not likely to lead to a career or long-term financial success.

In the next decades, the area would become even more saturated with additional attractions, which have placed even more strain on the inner core of Orlando and the city's surrounding suburbs. Disney World led to other parks that are not associated with Disney in any way, such as SeaWorld and Universal Studios Orlando. The city of Anaheim, though entirely taken up by Disneyland, has been largely engulfed by Los Angeles sprawl and has easy access to other industries and attractions. Orlando, like Coney Island, has an identity in the public mind that is entirely synonymous with the concept of the amusement park. Large hotels opened on the grounds of Disney World, as well as in other parts of Orlando.

Despite their desire to please the company, city officials occasionally found themselves at odds with Disney executives. Given how much power Roy and Walt had managed to secure from state officials, the company was virtually immune from nearly any governing policies that might have a negative impact on the park's bottom line. Work at the park may be satisfying and offer a chance to meet people from all over the world, but wages have typically been industry standard, if not lower. This causes problems for workers even in a state with a lower-than-average cost of living. Tying regional growth to tourism can also create issues during times of economic recession, when discretionary spending may be at an ebb. The environmental impact of having so many people in a single place has had a negative effect on the region's ecosystem. While the company undeniably continues to engage in efforts at environmental sustainability, the fact that so many guests travel a long way to get there means an overall increase in carbon dioxide emissions, as well as stresses on groundwater and air quality that may have a harsh impact on the area in the very long run.

What the company has done, however, is bring Florida to the world's attention in an indelible way. When people think about Florida in the modern era, they often do so through the lens that Disney has provided for them. The image of a happy place full of sunshine and places for families to enjoy together has undoubtedly benefited the state's residents by creating jobs and contributing to the tax base. The idea of plentiful sunshine, freedom, easy living, and fun originally drew even the morose Elias Disney there in the 19th century. Disney was unable to make a living in the Orlando area and had to return home, but his sons Walt and Roy made the state their own. It is to Disney that the state turns today for tax revenue, ideas, and the kind of overall family-friendly image they want to project to the entire United States and the rest of the globe. His two sons have taken the many ideas that Florida has held in the public imagination, updated them, and harnessed these concepts to the benefit of the Disney Company.

Since Roy's death, Disney World has seen yet more expansion and will probably continue to do so in the foreseeable future. The company has a lot of local land that remains undeveloped. Epcot came along in 1982. Other Disney parks under the umbrella of Disney World include Animal Kingdom, Hollywood Studios, and Typhoon Lagoon. The original park is known today as the Magic Kingdom. It's far larger than Disneyland and sprawls across a footprint that is likely to grow in a way Walt would have loved. Disney World is where the Disney brothers exercised their ultimate power. If it isn't quite what Walt, Roy, or the Floridian government officials had in mind in the late 1960s, it is one place that demonstrates how a single company can have a monumental impact on an American state.

Exporting America: EuroDisney and Beyond

In so many ways, Disney is a truly all-American company. The company has roots that began in Walt Disney's Midwestern childhood and then took flight as he and his brother found success. Together, he and his workers played a role in transforming the animation industry, rethinking amusement parks, turning Anaheim into a center for people on the West Coast to play, and bringing central Florida to worldwide attention and acclaim. Disney is part of the history of many facets of American life.

The company's influence has also spread beyond the shores of the United States. When *Steamboat Willie* first showed up in movie theaters across the globe, Europeans felt the same sense of delight that so enthralled audiences on the other side of the Atlantic. Mickey and Minnie Mouse quickly found success and an enormous audience eager for more and willing to pay for it. *Snow White and the Seven Dwarfs* was a huge hit across the globe. The Americans who flocked to see it ensured that the studio earned back the movie's huge production costs, but Europeans and moviegoers in other parts of the world brought in the profits the company needed to stay afloat. While World War II cut off some of the funds for the movies that the company produced, it also led to American government contracts that allowed the company to align itself with the idea of American patriotism and demonstrate that Disney was entirely devoted to the establishment's perceived American interests. In the coming decades, Disney movies and television shows found an international audience from the United Kingdom to Argentina and China.

As the company expanded even farther, Europeans and others took note. Disney World is especially popular with Europeans looking to escape their own grim northern winters. Just as officials in other parts of the United States wanted Disney to construct another Disneyland, the same was true for countries looking for something closer to home. For Disney officials and country business and community leaders in other parts of the world, there were many questions even before the first concepts of the park came into play. Perhaps the single most important was how to adapt the Disney vision to their own regional cultures. Several Disney parks have opened around the world since Disney World debuted. If such parks have not had the same impact on overseas locales from France to Hong Kong as they have had on California and Florida, they have undeniably provided a chance for the company to represent America to the global community. Entering a Disney park in another country is as close as many people in foreign countries will get to setting foot in the United States.

About a dozen years after Disney World opened, the first of the non-American parks opened in Tokyo in 1983. Within a few years, Tokyo Disneyland was a tremendous success, becoming the world's third-most-visited Disney theme park. Located about an hour outside Tokyo, Tokyo Disneyland combines Japanese culture with unabashed Disneyesque touches. The parking lot is much smaller, allowing people to rely on the nation's excellent rail connections. Most visitors are from Japan, with a small sprinkling of residents of other nations like nearby China and South Korea. Sleeping Beauty Castle has been renamed Cinderella Castle, but otherwise it serves to anchor the space visually and provide an immediate reference point for visitors. Other park areas are similar to Disneyland and Disney World, with rides like Big Thunder Mountain and Splash Mountain.

Like other Disney parks, Tokyo Disneyland offers food that combines American cuisine such as chicken and waffles with Japanese favorites such as mochi, filled gyoza buns, and berry milk tea. Also like other Disney parks, Tokyo Disneyland has expanded since the original opening. A second park, DisneySea, is now part of the entire complex. Of all the overseas parks, it is perhaps DisneySea that pays the most homage to the United States of Disney's early youth in Chicago. The American Waterfront port of call evokes turn-of-the-century New York City and Cape Cod, complete with an elevated railway and a historically authentic movie theater.

After years of negotiation and investigation, Disneyland Paris opened up 1992. Officials hoped that the central location, along with generous European vacation policies, would make a glowing combination. Like Tokyo Disneyland, the park is located roughly an hour from the city and can be reached by public transportation. As in Florida, park officials demanded concessions and subsidies from the government and got them. French government officials helped with the financing and local infrastructure necessary to connect it with the rest of the region. Unlike sunny Florida and California, the Parisian climate gets cold in the winter. However, despite what Disney Company officials believed when ruling out a park in the northern part of the United States, the cooler weather does not deter visitors. Even with reduced hours, people are happy to line up to enjoy Big Thunder Mountain in the snow.

As the only outpost of the company in Europe, Disneyland Paris embodies many ideas that Walt Disney held dear—and a few he didn't. Disneyland Paris is brighter and willing to go places Disney did not. The rides are scarier here, and the colors brighter. Little kids are allowed in, but the park also caters to people of many other age groups. The attractions are set in Bavarian villages and French inns and are about European heroes like Leonardo da Vinci and Jules Verne. Elegant details are lavishly carried out with the kind of intricacy that Disney aimed for in his original park. The European feel extends to smoking and drinking. Although the park does have dedicated smoking areas, smoking is tolerated everywhere. Wine is also widely available. This is one Disney park that retains strong ties to Parisian and European culture, with a certain casual attitude toward service that is at odds with the more attentive code in other parks.

As perhaps the biggest of all American experiences brought to European soil, the park manages to straddle both worlds without completely bringing either to life or entirely bridging the gap between the two. Many French cultural leaders continue to find Disneyland Paris out of step with the innate values of the French state. Ariane Mnouchkine, a world-renowned theater director, famously called the park a "cultural Chernobyl." Despite the occasional protests and a certain innate contempt for the very existence of formulaic Disney ideas, Disneyland Paris continues to be popular with Europeans in search of family-friendly attractions.

Two additional Asian parks round out the overseas Disney lineup. Of the two, Hong Kong Disneyland is much the smaller. With land reclaimed in one of the world's most crowded places, Hong Kong Disneyland lacks the sprawl of the company's American ventures. Four main areas, Adventureland, Fantasyland, Main Street, and Tomorrowland are the heart of the park, as in the American Disney parks. Grizzly Gulch, Mystic Point, and Toy Story Land were added later, with even more plans for expansion in the works. Elements of Chinese beliefs and culture can be seen everywhere. Many areas have been laid out in accordance with the Chinese design principle known as feng shui. The color red is abundant throughout the park, as it is associated with good luck in Chinese culture.

Chinese New Year gets as much attention from park officials as Halloween. The food also centers on Chinese food favorites, including Mickey red bean honey pudding, dumplings, and hot tea.

Planners at Shanghai Disneyland, the sixth Disney park, had plenty of history and experience to draw on when they opened it in 2011. Stung by criticism over aspects of Disneyland Paris, park officials sought to find ways to combine Chinese sensibilities while still keeping the essence of Disney and Americana alive for all their visitors. Like other overseas parks, this one can be reached by public transit. More than 24 million people have the ability to reach the park via train. The Haunted Mansion is gone in this particular park because of Chinese cultural reverence for ancestors and what would feel like mocking the dead. Squid and other seafood are featured prominently on the park's menus, along with venison and mapo tofu. The Garden of the Twelve Friends links Disney animals to the 12 animals of the Chinese zodiac. Mickey and Minnie are still there, along with a large castle, Fantasyland, and Tomorrowland. Shanghai Disneyland, perhaps more than any other overseas Disney park, is about bringing together two disparate communities and finding a commonly enjoyable experience.

These four parks directly represent America to over 1 billion people. Each demonstrates a certain evolution. There's a tightrope that Disney officials have attempted to walk carefully, but not always perfectly. Unlike Orlando, where the parks are the main regional attraction, each overseas Disney park is located in a much larger metro area, allowing easy reach for audiences in the millions via public transportation. At the same time, each overseas park must compete with other local attractions that are entirely unique to that city. Where officials have found their niche is with a distinctive combination of rides, shopping, dining, and cultural adaptations that combine family entertainment with the direct ability to experience a kind of American life, if only for a short time.

The merger of Disney, American cultural influence, and world pop culture is likely to continue as the company expands past its American base in search of new markets. What Disney officials have done is to create a fascinating union of American culture in places where the vast majority of residents will never spend any time in the United States. Each park is a mini-America open for business to the world. Disney parks outside the United States play an exclusive part in representing the country to places very far from its shores. Part cultural merger, part American embassy, and part simply a place to have a good time, the parks speak to many ideas at the same time.

CHAPTER FOUR

The Hat That Began It All: Spinoffs and Merchandise for Every Occasion

Few things are as ubiquitous as stuff with something Disney-related on it. From the Mickey Mouse hats of the 1950s, to the 1960s coonskin caps, to Disney princess dresses, to the Baby Yoda Lego sets of 2020, Disney things are in practically everyone's home. Kids love *Star Wars* action figures and Disney-related games, and adults go for the Disney Mickey Mouse waffle maker and the Disney villain wineglasses. Millions of people all over the globe have large and ever-expanding collections of Disney memorabilia. Some fans love detailed figurines and toys, while others line their jewelry boxes with pins and hang original art cels in the family room. Many fans eagerly anticipate getting the next Disney-related item almost as much as they wait for a new Disney film. Fans also create their own authorized and unauthorized versions of the stuff they see in their local Disney Store. Personally painted mugs and knitted scarves with a woven portrait of Mulan are just some of the ways people find to relate to the company's characters and creativity. Disney-related merchandise continues to play a large role in all that Disney does. Disney products also continue to bring in massive revenues that fuel the company's profits and help one of America's largest entertainment companies connect directly to its fans.

There's an almost natural feeling of progression from watching a film to thinking about the characters to the purchase of a related keepsake to take home. For many fans, it feels logical to buy a shirt, a pair of Mickey Mouse ears, or a tie to give at Father's Day as a reminder of a previous family visit to a Disney park. Disney's image appeals to kids and reminds adults of pleasant childhood memories.

This seemingly obvious marketing potential did not come to mind immediately during Disney's early filmmaking efforts. The idea that a company might profit by selling products related to one of its film was not readily apparent when Walt Disney dreamed up *Steamboat Willie*. One of the many things that Disney and his staffers did was to take the idea of a product tied to a performance or visiting a new place and raise it to a whole new level.

Mementos of travels and souvenirs from faraway places have a long history. People have always brought something home from their travels. Many people carelessly looted priceless treasures without a second thought. Where Disney brought something new to the table was in the sheer volume of material available to the public. Thanks to one man's concepts, marketing skills, and innate ability to understand the feelings of so many fans, Disney officials found not only a way to relate to their audience and enter their homes, but also to become one of the most recognized American brands, both at home and abroad.

In doing this, the company discovered a new and incredibly lucrative source of revenue. Cups with Minnie Mouse skirts, handbags with a Disney logo, and hand-built droids from *Star Wars* at Disneyland are not just secondary items put on shelves and then thrown away. Disney-related products have come to the company's financial rescue multiple times. In fact, Disney merchandise often served as the only profits the company earned on a movie or television show. With these products, Disney and his staffers not only created funds to help with the company's finances and pay back their shareholders, but they created a new way to bring movies to the public's attention. There's also been an expansion of copyright disputes, as Disney is quick to sue. In addition, their marketing efforts have left intriguing impressions for fans to mull over and make their own.

Disney showed other studios how to do the same for their own creative work. What was initially seen as a sideline business has become a routine way to market films to the public and recoup many if not most of the basic production costs, for all movie studios, not just Disney. A successful merchandising campaign can get a movie off the ground, finance other movies for a studio, and leave the audience thinking about the original campaign long after the initial run. Merchandising can also set up an ongoing relationship with the public that makes it easier to bring out sequels even years after the original project.

Movie merchandising can feel like a crude appeal for money for something of little intrinsic value. For many, however, products related to a movie or theme park also offer chances to transcend the boundaries between varied media. A painting of a Disney princess can inspire other artists to take the original concept of the character and put their own spin on it. In doing so, they show another viewpoint that can even improve on the original. Paintings of princesses with more realistic faces and women's bodies rooted in realistic body shapes pushed Disney animators to improve on their versions without compromising the company's fundamental artistry in the process. Many items once handed out in massive quantities have been recognized as vital pieces of American art and a part of the country's essential social and entertainment history. In good condition, original Disney-related merchandise can easily be resold for far more than the original retail price. Such items are then a form of investment, as well as a chance to participate in a classic American pastime. These are also items that are an intrinsic part of the world as it was during a single moment in time. Like the films and amusement parks, they reveal much about conditions of the era when they were made.

Herman "Kay" Kamen and Selling Mickey Mouse to the Public

Tying a product to a character or animation short for additional money began early in Walt Disney's career. Oswald the Lucky Rabbit had his own line of products for sale, including a stencil set and chocolate-covered marshmallows in his likeness. Shortly after *Steamboat Willie* came to theaters, Disney allowed Mickey Mouse to appear on a children's pencil set. This brought a much-needed $300 just for a single product, at a time when Disney was once again teetering on the edge of bankruptcy. Other offers came quickly after the item was a near-immediate hit. Roy Disney signed a deal with George Borgfeldt & Company in the early 1930s. The company sold figurines and other items based on Mickey and Minnie Mouse. In turn, Disney earned between 2.5 and 5 percent royalties on each item. Mickey also showed up in a syndicated comic strip, with royalties granted every time it ran.

These deals brought in a small direct infusion of cash at a time when the Disney brothers were thinking about the incredible possibilities inherent in color film. Further investigation revealed that the funding needed would probably be far beyond any project they'd done before. Roy and Walt also knew that the potential for much greater profits could lie in the use of images and other items tied to the popular Mickey and Minnie in some way.

A brash salesperson from New York City demonstrated just how large earnings could be if certain circumstances were met. Herbert "Kay" Kamen was the right person at the right time. He went on to show the Disneys exactly how to tap into this large audience with profits that would soon hit six figures and more. His brash personality and determination drastically increased the company's bottom line, took the Disney Company's drawings from the movie screen to people's homes, and transformed the entire movie industry. Thanks to Kamen, filmmakers found another often extremely lucrative funding outlet.

The man who would essentially remake the field of marketing for movies, television shows, and amusement parks was born in the multilayered Jewish community of New York City as Herman Samuel Kominetzky in 1892. Like Walt Disney, he grew up just as the movie industry was finding its footing. Much like Walt, he spent time in the Midwest and found it a congenial setting before moving on to sunny California. In a memorable bit of self-promotion that Disney would understand quite well, he dropped the plain Herbert and became Kay Kamen.

The reborn Kamen was very good at selling just about anything. He sold hats at first and then branched out into other things as his talent for sales became more obvious. Kamen began a marketing firm in Kansas City, Missouri. Kamen-Blair, his firm, was primarily about creating marketing campaigns for department stores. His personal creativity and inventiveness soon led to business in many other parts of the country. Kamen's work would come to the attention of Walt and Roy under circumstances that turned out to be extremely fruitful for both parties.

In 1930, the Disney brothers agreed to continue their contract with Borgfeldt even after their first initial success with *Steamboat Willie*. Unhappy with the anemic financial results, they allowed the company to sell only a handful of toys. By Christmas, it was obvious to both men that the company was simply not up to the task they had in mind. To their astonishment, even a poorly home-sewn Mickey Mouse doll did brisk business right before the holiday season, rapidly selling out far faster than expected. The brothers were deeply dissatisfied with the quality of the products that Borgfeldt were putting out, and even less happy with the extremely minor profits they were getting. The last thing either man wanted was shoddy items that would not stand up to heavy use and would make them look bad in the public eye when they fell apart. It was obvious that Borgfeldt was taking shortcuts and not living up to their initial agreement. So much effort had gone into the creation of the movies that it seemed foolish to sell Disney merchandise that was obviously inferior.

Just as attention to detail was the hallmark of the work the brothers put into their animation, the two wanted to see the same attention go into the products sold under the Disney name. Disney officials also realized that the timeline from the concept of a product to production was also far too long. That made it hard to capture audience enthusiasm and to reach fans during crucial gift-giving periods such as Christmas. Both brothers felt that there had to be other ways to deliver to their eager fans something that both children and adults would like. Their contract with Borgfeldt was ultimately lacking in the kind of energy and excitement that fans around the world were starting to expect from Disney.

Herman "Kay" Kamen stepped in to take charge. While some historians believe that it was he who made the first move, Neal Gabler, author of *Walt Disney: The Triumph of the American Imagination*, argues that it was Kamen's work in the field of department store marketing in Los Angeles that first caught Disney's attention. Walt contacted Kamen directly and asked him to come to Los Angeles as soon as possible. With the worldwide prestige and popularity now attached to the Disney name, this was the offer that Kamen had been waiting for all his life.

Kamen was not a particularly attractive man. Thick glasses and unruly black hair did not say Hollywood star, but there was an undeniable charisma to him. Underneath it all, he was very much like Walt, in that he was also completely at ease in other people's company. When the now-world-famous Walt Disney asked to meet with him, Kamen did not hesitate. He strode into Disney's office and immediately began to make bold promises. His ability to carry through with them would change the direction of the Disney Company, offer another way to make money, and make him personally a lot of money in the process.

Kamen knew he could make much more than the puny royalties Borgfeldt offered. Within the next 15 years, he presided over an empire of products that generated incredible sums of money. Kamen had Disney's approval and initial backing for a few basic plans at first. A short time later, it was obvious that Kamen was the right man for the job. His marketing had much in common with the new territory that the company was forging in the world of animated movies. Gone were the days of shoddy, hastily assembled products with little thought for the user beyond a quick profit. No more were the Disney-related items that took weeks just to get to market. In came masses of Disney merchandise that got into the public's hands quickly and yet still met the high standards that Disney had always aimed for in anything he brought to the public.

Kamen also did away with many minor companies attached to the Disney brand, as he believed that they did not bring the uniform marketing plan he had in mind. With kudos and money rolling in, the Disney Company's success made it apparent to him that larger and more prestigious names would be happy to be associated with Disney's brand in any way. Just as many widely respected and internationally known companies could hardly wait to sell directly to the public at Disneyland, they lined up to associate themselves with Mickey Mouse and Snow White. Mickey soon took his place in many American stores and homes. He went on cereal boxes, and then he went everywhere else. Proving that Disney could even reach into some of the most luxurious names in the world, Cartier sold diamond-studded Mickey Mouse bracelets. The public gobbled them up.

Like Disney, Kamen was willing to think in new ways about an industry that he would essentially develop in his own image. Unlike the employees at Borgfeldt, who were content with a handful of products, he saw opportunities everywhere. Less than a year after their initial meeting, Disney had over 40 licenses in place. By 1935, they were generating a great deal of money from sales all over the globe. Kamen opened up offices in New York City and over half a dozen cities overseas. He managed this astonishing achievement at the height of the Great Depression, when millions of people were out of work.

While audiences flocked to theaters to see Mickey Mouse again and again, even those who never saw a single frame of a Disney movie couldn't avoid Mickey's face. Nearly anything that could have Mickey Mouse on it did. Children had Mickey Mouse banks, where they kept their allowance. They could buy Mickey Mouse candy, get up in the morning to Mickey Mouse alarm clocks, head to school with a Mickey Mouse backpack, and spend recess playing with Mickey Mouse–themed balls. Dozens of Mickey Mouse toys, including Mickey Mouse boxing gloves, Mickey Mouse pull toys, Mickey Mouse drums, and Mickey Mouse baseballs, were part of the scene at playgrounds all over the United States. When it rained, then it was time to pull out a Mickey Mouse umbrella and put on your Mickey Mouse raincoat. Adults had their own merchandise line, just like kids. They played bridge with Mickey Mouse bridge favors, served food on Mickey Mouse chinaware, and carried purses with the Mickey Mouse logo. Minnie Mouse had her own line of gendered products for girls and women to use everywhere, from the car to the kitchen to the bathroom. Like Mickey Mouse, she was turned from a creature with plenty of moxie and a hint of spunk into a bland, vanilla character who could be used to project an image of docile 1930s femininity.

Mickey products were a gamble that might have easily fallen flat. Small-scale items had been marketed to the public before, but they were only a sideline at best. However, to Walt's astonishment and delight, Americans and people all over the world ran off to buy just about everything Disney and Kamen were selling. The classic Ingersoll Mickey Mouse watch, now acknowledged as a masterpiece of all-American design, led to a rush so deep the company had to stop advertising because it could not keep up with demand. The Manhattan branch of Macy's sold over 10,000 watches in a single day. Roy Disney proudly bought a dozen and kept them on hand for the rest of his life.

Kamen was behind it all. He and Walt Disney had an implicit understanding. Like Disney, he was someone unafraid to think hard and dream really big. Disney might spend hours instructing his animators on the proper way to draw Goofy or Doc, and he expected them to obey his precise commands. This did not apply to Kay Kamen. Kamen had free rein with all Disney marketing campaigns when it became clear that he knew exactly what he was doing. The partnership the two began in the early 1930s lasted until Kamen's tragic death in a 1949 airplane crash.

The year before he died, Kay Kamen sold over $100 million in Disney merchandise. After taxes and expenses, this only amounted to about $750,000. That is a fraction of the cost of a single animated movie. However, it provided a solid source of reliable new revenue for the company. Disney watchers wondered if Kamen had succeeded beyond Walt's wildest dreams, or if this was what he had expected all along. By 1934, the delighted studio head told people, according to historian Neal Gabler, that "he made more money from the ancillary rights to Mickey than from Mickey's cartoons." That was the year that "General Foods paid $1 million for the right to put Mickey Mouse cut-outs on the back of cereal boxes."

Before his death, Kamen would live to see an even greater expansion into new markets and opportunities for product tie-ins that are still very much a part of standard film studio operations today. He and Walt would learn from their successes. They would find new ways to give people something they didn't realize they needed or wanted until it showed up.

The 1930s were a phenomenal time for Disney products. A single book about Mickey Mouse sold over 2 million copies, making it one of the best-selling books of the entire decade. Kay Kamen had no problem charging exactly what he felt the market could bear. Mickey Mouse window displays might go for as much as $25,000. The English bought Mickey Mouse marmalade. The French found their own Mickey and Minnie china. It was clear not only that Mickey cartoons had global reach, but the same could be said of Mickey-related products.

By the end of the decade, both Australians and Canadians had 15 separate licenses to sell Disney products. Companies such as Ingersoll-Waterbury Clock Company and Lionel trains saw their profits soar based on selling a single Disney product. When Disney released *Snow White and the Seven Dwarfs*, a second round of Disney merchandising was ready to hand. An article in the *New York Times* on May 2, 1938, quoted Kay

Kamen as saying, "117 toy manufacturers have been licensed to use characters from 'Snow White.'" An Ohio factory employed workers around the clock to spend weeks making rubber dwarves. The article depicted Disney as many government officials and ordinary people saw it: as an engine of progress pulling the country out of economic depression. A 1935 editorial from the *New York Times* stated: "The fresh cheering is for Mickey the Big Business Man, the world's super-salesman. He finds work for jobless folk. He lifts corporations out of bankruptcy." Americans were bombarded with Disney things to buy almost everywhere they went, no matter what they did. Where some saw kitsch, millions more responded to the company's positive message in a decade that began with economic despair and ended in world war.

This would all begin to change in the following years. Disney products underwent rapid change in the 1940s as the company struggled to gear up for world war and a much-changed marketplace. *Snow White* was an immediate, incredible financial hit. Walt and company felt that this success proved that there was an enormous potential market for full-length animated features. The problem was that features took a great deal of money and many years of work to bring to the public. Nevertheless, the next decade saw a number of incredibly well made animated movies that would come to define Disney's public image even further. While the films made during this period are some of the best-loved films of all time, many of them were not a financial success. When many overseas markets closed because of war, it was harder for the company to break even, despite making incredibly high-quality movies. After releasing "155,000 shares of 6% convertible preferred stock" that brought in $3.8 million in 1940, Disney knew that there was an even greater market for his work from investors than with the general public.

This development made Disney a publicly owned company. It also put Disney on firmer financial footing. However, even this infusion of cash would not be quite enough to save them. World War II did that.

War changed the direction of the company's marketing efforts. U.S. government officials asked the Disney brothers to do their part, and they did. The government knew that this was one way to extend its global reach and get a pro-war message out to millions of people. Disney characters cheered on the war effort and seemed to embody the spirit that officials hoped to bring to soldiers, civilians, and the Allied Powers. The *New York Times* called Donald Duck an "ambassador-at-large, a salesman of the American Way." The National Museum of American History suggests, "By the end of the war, however, the title 'Salesman of the American Way' may well have belonged to Walt Disney himself." In addition to Mickey Mouse–related items that continued to sell well, there were materials from films like *Dumbo,* such as books and toys, that helped the company maintain a steady income stream. Company officials had another focus for the interpretation of their world via merchandise.

Marketing took the form of moral boosting for the troops. In-house animators crafted Disney characters and turned them into American art as they made highly individualized patches for over 1,000 units in the U.S. armed forces alone. Five people worked on these patches not only for service members in the United States, but for units that were part of the war effort abroad. The Women Airforce Service Pilots (WASP) of the British Royal Air Force had their own version of the American patches.

Meanwhile, Disney characters charged the American public with helping the war effort both at home and in other parts of the globe. From direct propaganda films to books and war bonds, Disney officials put their full marketing know-how into the war effort. There were buttons with Disney characters, and even war bonds bearing likenesses of the seven dwarves. In doing so, the company became synonymous with the very idea of American patriotism in the public mind all over the globe. As Elizabeth Segran of *Fast Company* points out, "The character was so tied to war efforts that the name 'Mickey Mouse' was a password for an important high-level briefing about a week before D-Day, at a British naval base on the English Channel."

Despite these efforts, the company earned very little money from the proceeds. These were not Mickey Mouse watches or other products that could bring in $600,000 in a single year, as Kay Kamen had done soon after Disney hired him. Over the next few years, Disney felt adrift. Marketing revenues fell even as the company churned out films. Movies like *Cinderella, Alice in Wonderland,* and *Peter Pan* offered a mix of muted critical and financial success.

In 1949, the company created a brand-new department. The character-merchandising division even began by marketing products to the public well before a film's release. Even before *Cinderella* was seen by the public, fans found themed products to purchase during the holiday shopping season, including their own glass slippers. With the rise of a new medium, Disney's marketing efforts would once again lift its finances and end up sparking another revolution in how marketing for films and television shows would be brought to the American public.

Coonskin Caps and Mickey Mouse Ears

Disney came to the world's attention by creating appealing animation that people had never seen before and pushing the boundaries of the art form itself. By the 1950s, a new medium was about to take the world by storm, just as animation had done a generation earlier. Unlike many of his fellow filmmakers, Walt Disney took television very seriously. In the late 1940s, he spent a week in New York City immersing himself in the technology. He was sure that there was a massive audience just waiting for him yet again on those tiny, black-and-white screens. Two television specials in the early 1950s marked the beginning of Disney's start in what would become a brand-new but highly effective outlet for him. Television executives wanted him on board as much as he wanted to be there with them. ABC rushed to offer his company a huge contract. With their help, he was not only tied to the network, but he was in the lives of millions of Americans each week.

The contract with ABC served two purposes. The first allowed the nation's third-ranked network to distinguish itself in the public mind with a well-known, beloved, long-established, and wholesome American company. The second gave Disney almost previously unimagined access to the American public and a chance to influence how the public saw him. Walt Disney wanted exposure, but he also wanted funding for his new amusement park, Disneyland. To that end, he needed a lot of money. While the park would later prove to be a major source of revenue, buying the land he craved in California meant reaching deep into his own personal pockets. The contract with ABC was lucrative, but that was only the start. Production costs for the kind of programming that Disney intended to bring to the public were steep. Even with help from ABC and eager advertisers, it was not clear that television could come to his financial rescue. Once again, spin-off products were there to help. By the time Disneyland was ready to welcome the public, a chunk of the costs for the park came not just from the studio and the network, but also in part from the Disney brand merchandise the public bought.

Disney was a huge hit on television from practically the first moment *Davy Crockett* aired. His show's ratings trounced nearly every single thing on television, even in repeats. Within a short time, the Disney Company was responsible for nearly half of ABC's advertising revenue. Like the money that Disney earned from movies, this was a huge chunk of change. But, like the movies, Disney was also facing immense production costs for his television creations. On December 5, 1954, Walt's birthday, the company brought the first of multiple installments of a miniseries on Davy Crockett to the public. As usual, Disney poured money into the miniseries. The first three episodes alone cost almost $750,000 to bring to the small screen.

Kamen had taught Walt Disney well. *Davy Crockett* was an instant hit. Disney was surprised, but he and his company were ready and waiting with merchandise to go along with the series. Kids loved Davy Crockett, and so did their parents. Once again, Disney rolled out stuff to buy everywhere people went. There were books, jackets, lunch boxes, and dolls. Kids could go to bed in Davy Crockett pajamas and play with harmless Davy Crockett knives on weekends.

The hot toy that year was a Davy Crockett coonskin cap. Retailing for $2.98, boys and girls wore them everywhere. A total of 10 million were sold within weeks after the first show. Some were made of real raccoon skins, while others were made of anything from rabbit to skunk. Neither the kids nor the adults cared. According to the *New York Times* in 1955, "products keyed to the song's theme are expected to ring up cash registers to the tune of $300,000,000 by the end of this year." That's over $2 billion in today's money. Once again, the company had caught on to a trend and found ways to exploit it financially.

As it turned out, 40 million Americans, or one in four, watched at least one episode of the five-part series. Disney would make back all the costs for the series and more when it released the series in theaters as a single movie and brought in $2.5 million. The company earned even more money from Davy Crockett merchandise. In a few short weeks, Disney changed the way that television producers looked at the costs of making a show. While advertising revenue continued to play a part in how programs were financed, it was clearly not the only game in town. Disney officials taught television executives that they could do the same thing with television shows that Disney had done with his film characters: leverage them to make money.

In the aftermath of this immense and almost wholly unexpected success, ABC officials essentially pleaded with Disney to bring them additional programs. They wanted an hour a day, five days a week. Once again, Disney decided children's programming was the way to go. The success of the *Davy Crockett* series indicated that there was a market for children's programming. Kids were likely to sit still after school and watch television, and parents had faith that Disney would offer trustworthy entertainment.

After a lot of careful planning, Disney and his staffers came up with one of those shows, which would make a vast impact on the lives of American children. Dubbed *The Mickey Mouse Club,* the show was designed to capture kids' attention after school. The series was essentially a mishmash of everything from a talent show to a children's newsreel to a daily cartoon. Walt Disney played a basic role and then stepped back. He picked the original Mousekeeteers, including Annette Funicello and Frankie Avalon, and showed up on the set during filming to show them what he wanted. The critics hated it. The *New York Times* called the show, "irritating cute," and "bereft of any semblance of the justly famous Disney touch." Parents and kids didn't care.

From 1955 to 1959, Disney aired nearly 400 episodes to a substantial audience. Three new versions of the show followed in the next decades. *The New Mickey Mouse Club* aired from 1977 to 1978, featuring a more diverse cast. *The All-New Mickey Mouse Club* was a major show on the Disney Channel. Aimed at teens rather than preteens, no one wore the ears when it ran from 1989 to 1994. *Club Mickey Mouse,* the latest incarnation, began in 2017 and can be found on Facebook and Instagram. On the show, eight new Mouseketeers have adventures and sing songs that kids can watch any time they like. Merchandise such as team jackets and songs and videos that bring in advertisers and fans are on hand yet again.

Disney also eventually spurred parents to advocate for improvements in the quality of the programming presented to their children. Parents were understandably dismayed at the quality of the programming that Disney was presenting to their children on the small screen. They liked the history behind Davy Crockett, but other shows lacked the same sense of history and overall quality. The overt ties to product lines did little to offer kids and parents much beyond songs and cartoons. Many parents and advocacy groups ultimately became worried about the commercialization of a medium that had initially seemed harmless.

By the late 1960s, a grassroots organization known as Action for Children's Television asked television officials to do better. The organization wanted to reduce the amount of time children were spending in front of the screen and the products being marketed to them. Unhealthy foods laden with fat and sugar often took center stage during commercials, while violence was presented as a normal part of the day. Within a decade, the organization was both lobbying against the unrelenting violence in television programming aimed at children and demanding that network television officials decrease their direct merchandising to children.

In response to this movement, network executives and parents began to explore other avenues. High-quality children's programming such as *Schoolhouse Rock, Captain Kangaroo, Sesame Street,* and *Mister Rogers' Neighborhood* expanded the role that Disney had sought out. Children's shows aimed to help children understand the world around them by teaching them basic academic subjects such as reading, writing, math, science, and social studies. When Ronald Reagan was elected president in 1980, the process of expanding the quality of children's television programming hit a setback. His policy of deregulation extended to the marketplace on television, leading to the rise of what became known as the merchandise-driven show. In essence, these shows were half-hour commercials intended to do little more than sell toys.

Since that time, the Federal Communications Commission (FCC) has cracked down on the kind of programming that can be presented to preschoolers, children, and teens. The Children's Television Act of 1990 placed a series of restrictions that broadcasters must follow when working on programming aimed at kids 16 and younger. Rules were put in place requiring advertisers to maintain boundaries between a television show and its advertisers. The amount of time that could be devoted to advertising during a show was also limited. Since then, parents and children's advocacy groups have continued to lobby for further regulating the way that information is presented to those under 18. Disney began a process that remains an ongoing source of debate. The tug between educating children on television, entertaining them, and treating them as mere consumers is a line that Disney has set up—and crossed—many times.

While these changes would come later, the original version of *The Mickey Mouse Club* took parents largely off guard. Disney's intensely upright image remained very much in the public eye. Programming with Disney's name on it and with his obvious backing was left largely unscrutinized during this time. For him, the show, like much of what was presented to the public at this time, really had one aim: to get the funds he needed for his dream park. Unfortunately for his company, Walt Disney once again underestimated the costs of making a show for the network. The only reason he stuck with the series is because ABC officials agreed to add over $2 million as a sweetener.

Not only did the show bring viewers to Disneyland, but *The Mickey Mouse Club* rapidly became yet another outlet for the sale of merchandise. Just like Davy Crockett, a single product would linger in the public mind and enter classic American design. Disney staff writer Roy Williams came up with the idea of a black felt cap with plastic mouse ears on the sides. In doing so, he wanted to give all the members of the show a uniform look that was easily visible, even in black and white. Fans quickly began to clamor for their own version of the hat. Disney officials responded just as rapidly as they had when it came to their original Mickey Mouse merchandise. Benay-Albee Novelty Company was chosen to bring the caps to the public, selling them at Disneyland. Over the next few months, the soft, folded black hats took their place alongside the coonskin cap and the Mickey Mouse watch: a must have for millions of Americans.

Within weeks, Mickey Mouse ears became the single most instantly recognizable Disney symbol. The public wore them in the park and wore then at home. Kids brought them to parties and wore them when they watched Disney shows. Over the following decades, the Mickey Mouse hat evolved into a blank slate from which to project almost anything else the public had in mind. The standard black, white, and red gave way to any shade imaginable. Colors like neon pink and ultraviolet became an inventive twist on the black version. Babies have their own, with a simple chin strap. Adults have larger sizes that fit equally well. Hundreds of official and unofficial versions have flooded the market since the first items were sold to the public. People made their own, and they bought them too. The original thick felt cap eventually evolved into a basic outline with merely a headband with sparkly ears and a bow in the middle. They're easier to wear in the Florida humidity and California heat.

Once again, Disney made the decision to jump on the marketing bandwagon as soon as possible. Disney gave designers permission to experiment with the form, shape, and color of the Mickey Mouse ears. In the years since the Mouseketeers wore them, many limited-edition versions have been issued, and many more have become collector's items. There's a pair of ears for just about every occasion. One pair was designed to celebrate the 40th anniversary of the Haunted Mansion. Offered to the public on September 30, 2011, they sold out a short time later. The release of the live-action film of Disney's *Alice in Wonderland* was accompanied by 500 Mickey ears in black and green, which were grabbed up as quickly as they hit the shelves. When Disneyland celebrated its 50th anniversary in 2005, officials brought out a gold version of the hat retailing for $80. The standard version, complete with cap and stapled plastic ears, can still be found in mass retailers for a few bucks. Today, Disney officials have over 200 different kinds of hats that can be found all over the globe. More upscale versions include a limited edition of 50 hats that are sold online for hundreds of dollars and boast details like crystals sewn on by hand. Underneath it all continues an essential shape that will always evoke Disney. One glimpse of the curved ears, and we all know exactly what we're seeing.

Disney Marketing since Walt

Over the course of his time with the company he founded, Walt was often asked precisely what he did. Those at *Walt Disney News Today* ultimately summarized his role in a single paragraph:

> Responding to a question posed by National Geographic, Walt Disney described in this way his role as the company's creative catalyst: "You know, I was stumped one day when a little boy asked, 'Do you draw

The Hat That Began It All

Mickey Mouse?' I had to admit I do not draw anymore. 'Then you think up all the jokes and ideas?' 'No,' I said, 'I don't do that.' Finally, he looked at me and said, 'Mr. Disney, just what do you do?' 'Well,' I said, 'sometimes I think of myself as a little bee. I go from one area of the studio to another and gather pollen and sort of stimulate everybody.' I guess that's the job I do." While he was alive, Walt Disney was the driving force behind what the company did.

In the aftermath of Walt Disney's quick death from lung cancer in his mid-sixties, company officials used this time to take stock of Walt's vision. Over the next decades, company officials used varying strategies to stay in touch with their customer base, expand into newer markets, and find ways to keep the Disney name in the news. Company leaders often felt a tug of war between the chaste image the company projected to the public and the reality that the market for their product limited their ability to remain both profitable and cutting-edge. At the heart of their plans were two essential ideas: making new movies and bringing people to the company's amusement parks. Walt spent much of his later years attempting to get Disney World off the ground. When he died, it was left to his younger brother Roy to step up. By early 1970, Disney World was open for business. What would follow after he died was, many felt, highly formulaic and lacking in creative energy.

Many industry insiders and those watching the company from afar did not like what they saw. George Lucas, the man behind the *Star Wars* franchise, believed that the company pulled back from the market it had essentially created. He said, "Disney had abdicated its reign over the children's market," according to an account in *Easy Riders, Raging Bulls: How the Sex-Drugs-and-Rock 'n' Roll Generation Saved Hollywood* by Peter Biskind, "and nothing had replaced it." He and many others found Disney's movies predictable and all too reliant on marketing rather than creativity. "This is a Disney movie," Lucas told his own investors, according to the Biskind book. "All Disney movies make $16 million, so this movie is going to make $16 million. It cost $10 million, so we're going to lose money on the release, but I hope to make some of it back on the toys."

Movies from this time relied on bland and predictable plotlines that fit into the existing oeuvre rather than expanding it. Audiences showed up, but the company was no longer the industry leader it had once been. By the end of the decade, company officials argued about where to go without compromising the company's fundamental brand. As the early 1980s began, they made the decision to aim for an older audience. Disney's son-in-law, Ron Miller, argued that it was time to push for the PG market because he believed, as he said in an interview, "there appears to be a lid on our product. The age group we typically appeal to just won't give us the big attendance numbers that some other studios get." The very notion of a Disney movie with a PG rating was startling and bizarre to many at the studio and many of their fans. The result was sometimes acclaimed and sometimes bizarre and simply bad. Pulitzer Prize–winning movie critic Roger Ebert called *Million Dollar Duck*, "one of the most profoundly stupid movies I've ever seen." *The Black Hole*, a movie with many dark scenes, won some respect even as audiences found the work unappealing, especially compared with other science fiction movies. With a $20 million price tag, the movie managed to make a profit, but scientists condemned the premise and execution. Movies like *Tron* and *The Black Cauldron* had intense themes that Disney had shied away from over the course of his career. Many later became cult favorites just as *Pinocchio* and *Fantasia* had in previous decades. Audiences were left confused about the direction of the company and what to expect from a Disney movie. It was not until the 1990s that the company again gained respect for their contemporary products with a series of widely admired animated features, including *Aladdin* and *Beauty and the Beast*.

Part of the process of marketing at this point was figuring out how to deal with the nascent home video market. By the mid-1980s, about half of all homes had a video cassette recorder (VCR). The VCR meant that people no longer had to buy a ticket and go to a movie theater. They could also buy copies of their favorite movies for repeated viewing. Once again, the spur of a new technology would prove to be a catalyst for company operations. It would also change the face and process of movie marketing. During the 1970s and early part of the following decade, company officials reissued animated classics like *Cinderella* and *Dumbo* in theaters roughly every 7 to 10 years. Their goal was to bring in a brand-new audience while keeping some of the most beloved of all Disney Company movies locked up and out of the public eye. Once people could purchase or rent their movies whenever they wanted, company officials were worried that this provided little incentive for them to head to the movie theater.

Disney executives also had to decide if they wanted to release such classics for good, and if so, what would be a fair price. *Pinocchio* proved to be a test case that would set the standard for the company's other movies and plans to tap into the home movie rental and purchase markets. Originally priced at $79.95, the price was later dropped to $29.95 in 1985 when many video rental prices refused to stock it at the higher price. Over 600,000 copies were sold a short time later to individuals as well as stores.

Next up was *Sleeping Beauty*. Officials calculated that releasing it four times over the next three decades would lead to $125 million in box office sales, while selling it in the home video market at the same price as *Pinocchio* would bring in $100 million. The first plan allowed for immediate income to fuel additional projects, while the second might give them cash to fuel additional projects. Under the tagline, "Bring Disney Home for Good," a massive $7 million marketing campaign fueled sales of more than 1.3 million copies and made it one of the most profitable of all Disney ventures. Worries about the potential cheapening of the brand were swept away. The company's chief executive officer (CEO), Michael Eisner, explained to shareholders, "The best possible impact on our brand turned out to be having our classic films in people's homes, where they were watched over and over."

The 1990s saw further expansion into the home video market. Disney officials turned to computer animation techniques to provide a revamped *Fantasia* with better color and sound. The film sold 15 million copies after the first release in 1991. *Snow White* followed in 1994. It, too, sold extremely well as 50 million consumers scooped it up. Over the next decades, Disney officials turned to DVDs and saw yet more profits for the movies in the vault. The company's Walt Disney Home Video brand also pioneered the process of releasing movies aimed at the rental market rather than widespread theatrical release. Starting with *The Return of Jafar* in 1994, hundreds of shorts and what amounted to prequels and sequels were made available to the home consumer. With titles like *Mulan II* and *Beauty and The Beast: The Enchanted Christmas*, these were not full-length features. Much like many of the shorts Disney did during the 1930s and 1940s, critics continue to find some worthy of note, while others were merely derivative.

Marketing for Disney's theme parks also went in a slightly different direction. The parks continue to be advertised as the ideal destination for a family trip. Millions of parents brought their kids to an ever-expanding space with new attractions for a new generation. At the same time, just as officials had seen a new market for adults in Disney films, they saw the same potential when it came to their theme parks and adult audiences. Marketing experts expanded their efforts to draw in singles and couples without children.

In 1989, officials opened the Pleasure Island complex in Downtown Disney. Aimed at adults, the complex brought in locals as well as tourists. Multiple attractions just for adults included several dance clubs, comedy clubs, shopping outlets, restaurants, and bars. Over the next three decades, the area went through multiple changes. In the end, this led to a more family-focused experience rather than one largely designed for adults. Areas such as Disney Springs and The BoardWalk still continue to offer nightclubs, alcoholic drinks, and other adult-themed entertainment options, and children take second place. Couples looking for a romantic dining option can turn to many world-class dining possibilities that discourage younger visitors. Other activities such as backstage tours actually prohibit visitors under a certain age. Festivals like the Epcot International Food and Wine Festival also bring in an older crowd.

The strategy of marketing to adults spread to other amusement parks and venues aimed originally at children. Disney rival Universal Studios added the slogan, "Kids grow up. So do vacations." Disney and other parks also encourage seniors to visit by offering discount tickets, along with amenities such as handicapped parking and special seating during shows. Now, by the second decade of the twenty-first century, such efforts have begun to pay off. More than half of all Walt Disney World visitors are adults without kids. Adults are drawn there because it offers a venue to rekindle fond childhood memories and an opportunity to participate in a familiar and comforting experience.

CHAPTER FIVE

Princesses, Politics, and a Different Audience: Controversies That Continue to Challenge Perceptions Today

Like many classic American brands, Disney is many things to many people. The company is a renowned vacation destination, a movie-making juggernaut, and an immensely creative force in the lives of many Americans and people across the globe. Whether watching *Hamilton* at home on Disney+, asking a bartender for a Baby Yoda martini, or making plans to visit Disneyland Paris, Disney continues to have vast and intense reach. Walt Disney was undeniably a man of genius and daring. He began his life in total obscurity and ended it as a beloved figure to people all over the world. The company's achievements in his name are many and varied. His work and the work of his animators in the 1920s and 1930s took American animation and the entire world of animation by storm in a relatively short time span. Historians credit the company with many innovations that have had an impact on the lives of Americans of all ages. The synchronization of drawings and sound, along with fully fleshed-out storylines, transformed the entire animation industry and upped audience expectations. Techniques that the company used and developed also became an integral part of the work of animators. He standardized animation techniques for the entire industry. Florida is a different place in part because of Disney World and Roy's decision to implement his brother's plans. What was once a small animation studio is today a huge enterprise that continues to reach into many facets of

American life. Each day, people read the pages of *National Geographic* and Marvel comics. They watch old movies from Disney+, tune into Hulu and ESPN, and get in long lines to enjoy the latest ride at Epcot. Disney does business in many countries around the world, from Japan and France to Argentina, and the name instantly evokes the United States as both a source of leading-edge ideas and many familiar, comforting fictional worlds.

Beneath the shiny, pretty surface lies a complicated history that touches on many aspects of the lives of women and deserves to be thoroughly told and understood. While Disney gave one woman a major role in the design of his works and the iconic It's a Small World After All ride, his depiction of women in his work was often stilted and oppressive. Despite being the doting father of two daughters, Walt Disney saw women and girls as little more than marriage and childbearing material in his own life. Since his death, it has literally taken decades for Disney officials to show us fully realized, memorable female characters. For those in search of a more complicated American history where issues of race are openly discussed, company officials have done little to advance this much-needed dialogue. In many instances, Disney has offered incredibly offensive and deeply racist stereotypes that gloss over American history and do a vast disservice to viewers.

Efforts to remedy this unappealing history remain an ongoing process. Much the same can be said of the way that the company treats its employees. Working at Disney still has well-documented hazards, including recent allegations that company officials have done little to protect workers from the spread of COVID-19. Many company workers are underpaid and have jobs offering little chance at promotion or better pay. The company continues to have an influence on Florida's laws and how the state is run, making it hard to lobby for change.

Walt Disney was not only a product of his time, but he was also someone who shaped how people during much of his adult life thought about themselves and the world around them. He often brought out the very worst of American instincts, even as he preached a world of unity and innocence. In the middle of movies that make people smile even today, there are moments that showcase almost unconscious biases and make it hard to view movies like *Fantasia* without cringing once certain facts are made known. Disney officials have done much to move past the legacy that Walt left them. In the process, they have brought out a better, more rounded, and loving version of the worlds that he first set in motion.

Helpless Females, Male Rescues, and Happily Ever After: Life for Women in Disney Films

Mickey Mouse has Minnie Mouse. Snow White has her seven dwarves and a prince who comes to her rescue in the end. Cinderella has a fairy godmother and a devoted group of mice to help with her menial household chores. She sits there waiting for her own prince to come along and remove her from the world of household drudgery. It's hard to think of the world of women in many Disney films without conjuring up images of helpless young women sitting around, longing for a man to show up and do things for them. The prince is primarily there to save the passive heroine from a community that doesn't value her. The essential Disney girl/woman is a young and pretty damsel in some form of immediate and long-term distress. Even when the prince isn't around to serve as the center of the movie, often other, supposedly more competent characters are around to watch over her children and keep house because she can't. She's not particularly good at anything in most instances, nor is she supposed to be.

The Disney heroine of Walt's vision has a role, and that role is to be around for the boys and the men in her life. Once they're finished doing what has to be done, she serves as the prize to be won in the end. Her reward is the chance to live happily ever after. Happily ever after amounts to marriage to the right man, and then a rosy future where she doesn't have to make beds and cook for men or seven dwarfs. Marriage is her ultimate destiny. Marriage is where she can come into her own. In Disney films, marriage is usually where the tale ends. We don't know what's going to happen when the heroine is done participating in her adventures beyond heading to the altar.

Disney movies show only a handful of married women in any substantial role. Motherhood, on the other hand, is often seen in a negative light. Disney's movies bring us some loving parents, but few competent parents. Mary Poppins takes over child care and other mundane tasks as the dream nanny. By turns warm, sweet, and demanding, she is the substitute parent that the kids cherish. Meanwhile, Winifred Banks is far too busy fighting for women's suffrage to attend to her own children's needs. When mothers are on screen, they are often helpless to protect their offspring. Bambi's mom dies. Dumbo's mom cannot save him from being taken away from her. Even in later works like *Mulan* and *The Lion King*, moms do little to protect their children from danger. Stepmothers who pose a serious threat to the main characters are also widely present in Disney films. They form the basic plotlines of *Snow White* and *Cinderella*. Fathers are presented as equally hapless parents, but they are largely spared the experience of being stepparents actively working against an innocent child's interests for no other reason other than lack of direct blood ties.

Not until the 1990s did Disney Studios began to break free of the world of girls and women forced to molder in sexist, gendered roles. Even in this context, the women in many Disney films are largely vehicles for male desires. *Aladdin* has a plucky heroine with a great deal of charm and a willingness to break boundaries, but Aladdin does most of the work while Jasmine sits around and waits for him. The clever Belle of *Beauty and the Beast* reads books and has an interior life of her own. She seems to be going somewhere where she'll have a role to play beyond that of household ornament. But Belle still needs rescuing from a pack of wolves by the Beast as much as he needs her to love him and free him from a wicked spell. The heroines in Disney movies are largely passive actors, even when they're the center of the story. They serve to frame the story of the male hero rather than directly participating in most of the action on screen.

Within such narrow parameters, the company occasionally steps over the lines they set up and lets women be the authors of their own fate. In *Sleeping Beauty*, the beautiful heroine is the star of the show in her own right. Much of the action, however, centers on the three good fairies at her side, ready for action. Flora, Fauna, and Merryweather mitigate the worst effects of the evil fairy's spell. As older women, they are free of the need to look pretty and attract the attention of a handsome prince merely to have a place at the table. In her book *Good Girls and Wicked Witches: Women in Disney's Feature Animation*, author Amy M. Davis makes the essential point that Disney assumed a certain role in the life of many Americans during his lifetime. He was arguably the person who did the most to tell Americans the kind of tales that had once been passed along to children as part of the local and national culture. In taking on a quasi-parental role, Disney looked to the world of fairy tales for a great deal of his inspiration. Familiar tales allowed an immediate audience connection. Fairy tales, while allowing the use of imagination, are also traditionally limited by stereotypes and highly sexed roles. They offer stories, but there's little that challenges the existing society around them in any substantive way. Disney created worlds in which tales like these are fully realized, but he accepted the essence of the stories. Much of his early work makes use of fables and is all about children. His company still plays that role for many American children. Young Americans and their counterparts around the world begin to think about what they might want from life by watching his movies and other outlets such as the Disney Channel. They watch *Finding Nemo*, *Monsters Inc.*, and *Cars* with mom and dad. Classic sexism, in which the hero does things while the heroine watches, is quite common in the tales that Disney tells. It is only long after Disney's death that the company has begun efforts to get out of this frustrating, sexist straitjacket.

Amy M. Davis points to characters such as Ariel in *The Little Mermaid* to prove her point. Ariel is extremely curious about the world around her, and that motivates her actions as much as love. Even though in real life, Pocahontas was forced to marry an Englishman and go to the United Kingdom against her wishes, in the Disney film she stays home and takes a leadership role in her society. In *Brave*, produced under the direction of Pixar Animation Studios and then released and distributed by Walt Disney Pictures, the heroine, Merida, stands up for herself and winds up ultimately controlling her own destiny. Many critics hailed the movie for centering a female character and her relationships with others. However, the film's own director, Brenda Chapman, called out the studio for moving away from the film's attempt to present a realistic-looking female character with frizzy hair and a normal body type. Chapman argued that Disney turned her into the studio's standard big-eyed Barbie doll. In doing so, she felt that the studio undermined the essential message of the movie: girls can have normal bodies and still have adventures and the respect of their society.

Two years later, in 2013, Disney finally found a voice for girls that did not revolve around men. *Frozen* presents a conscious attempt to rethink the role of female lead. The two main characters, Elsa and Anna, are sisters. Even though both sisters are royal and conventionally pretty, the main story centers on the relationship between the two rather than ultimate redemption by a male lead.

Many other issues are readily apparent when taking a closer look at the role of women and girls in Disney's films. A 2016 *Washington Post* article asked, "Why are characters so obsessed with Snow White's looks? Why doesn't Cinderella have any talents or hobbies? And why doesn't Sleeping Beauty do anything besides get drugged and await rescue?" The same article talks about the role of dialogue in many Disney movies, citing the fact that "all of the princess movies from 1989–1999—Disney's 'Renaissance' era—are startlingly male-dominated. Men speak 71% of the time in *Beauty and the Beast* (1991); 90% of the time in *Aladdin* (1992); 76% of the time in *Pocahontas* (1995)."

Other authors have brought issues regarding the presentation of women in Disney's films to the forefront. Girls and women elevated to the role of heroine in Disney films are pretty, or at least highly attractive in some way. They fit the conventions of female beauty, with long, flowing hair, hourglass figures, and entirely smooth complexions. The Disney heroine never has a zit or acne scars. She has no extra body fat. This is largely the source of her essential usefulness and desirability to the male hero. That is mostly what matters in Disney movies. Pretty women exist as objects for men to find and love. They have almost no need to develop other qualities such as intelligence, bravery, or strength. A pretty girl in the Disney canon will find love and be loved in turn. She might have other qualities, such as a love of books or a desire for adventure, but in the end the fact that she is pretty is her most important quality. The ugly stepsister can only watch in frustration. She is a female consigned to either utterly evil villain or left to live out her days as a spinster, sitting on the sidelines and watching her pretty stepsister reap the rewards of her loveliness. Disney films continue to struggle with the realistic presentation of girls' bodies to boys and girls. Very long hair, big, wide-set eyes, tiny noses, and very thin bodies with tiny hips are the norm. When a female character deviates from the standard pretty formula, this presents certain cues to the audience. Such a character is likely to play a secondary role, or even the role of the female villain as the action unfolds. She will probably not have a happy life in the movie or indeed her entire life when the movie is done.

Examining the role of girls and women on screen tells us much about the role of women that Disney films present to the world. It is behind the scenes, in the day-to-day workings of the studio, where reality was far more complicated. In some ways, Walt Disney allowed women a role, while in other ways, he actively worked against them. Disney made several attempts to promote the work of women animators. As his studio began to grow, he sought out more employees of all backgrounds. Like many other employers at the time, Disney called the women who worked for him "girls" when the men remained "men." He and many other employers thought of women as merely secondary to men.

Within the studio, there were lots of different jobs. Some positions were more prestigious and earned more money. One particular division was between the paint-and-ink workers and the higher-level animators. Paint-and-ink workers did a lot of drudge work. Their role was all about cleaning up the work that others did rather than creating ideas of their own. Animators had the freedom to create their own work, so long as it met Disney's standards. Nearly every single worker in the paint-and-ink division was female, while most animators were men. Women who applied for a position at Disney were cautioned, "Women do not do any of the creative work in connection with preparing the cartoons for the screen, as that task is performed entirely by young men." Those who persisted were further told, "It would not be advisable to come to Hollywood. . . . There are really few openings in comparison with the number of girls who apply."

At the same time, Disney made it clear that he did not necessarily consider the women who worked at the studio inferior because they were women. When war began in Europe, many male employees at the studios were concerned that women would take their places when they went to fight, which would lower their salaries. In a staff speech given in February 1941, Disney responded to such concerns with a mixed message. On one hand, he said, "The girl artists have the right to expect the same chances for advancement as men, and I honestly believe that they may eventually contribute something to this business that men never would or could." He also singled out three female employees for special praise: Ethel Kuslar, Sylvia Holland, and Retta Scott. Kulsar and Holland worked on several films, including *Fantasia*. Scott would later become the first female animator given credit after the release of *Bambi*. On the other hand, he talked of women in his company in terms of their ability to stand in for the male workers at the studio while the men went to war. He did not view the work that the women did as vitally important or a chance to advance the parameters of animation. Women at Disney Studios, like the female characters he showed on screen, were there to play a supporting role, while the men took the well-paying jobs and did most of the acclaimed and far more valued creative work.

Over the next two decades and beyond, Disney Studios was simultaneously a place where women could watch their careers unfold and a place where they participated in efforts that presented the ideal of homemaker as the ultimate goal for girls. In her book *The Queens of Animation: The Untold Story of Women Who Transformed the World of Disney and Made Cinematic History*, author Nathalia Holt brings the history of women's contributions to Disney work to the public's attention. Women were often given little official recognition for the work they did at Disney. As the credits roll along at the end of *Snow White*, only two women, Hazel Sewell and Dorothy Ann Blank, are named at all, despite the fact that many women worked on the movie in some capacity. In the new few years, Disney attempted to increase the number of women working at his company. The department even circulated a memo stating that "it has always been Walt's hope that the studio could be a place where girls can be employed without fear of embarrassment or humiliation." Despite these assertions, many barriers remained. Just to get hired, women had to be especially good at their craft. Many male Disney employees viewed animation as an exclusively male province.

By the early 1940s the studio employed more than 1,000 workers, over 300 of whom were women. As World War II appeared to loom on the horizon and funds for the movies began to dry up, Disney Studios faced multiple operating challenges. The first was Disney workers striking for more money. Many felt underpaid and overworked. They felt that striking was the only way to change their working conditions. The second was vastly reduced cash reserves, as animated movies flopped financially even as the studio won praise. Disney responded to the company's problems by going public, only to find its stock price tumbling quickly. He also responded to the needs of his creditors by laying off many people and focusing on work for the government once the war began. Women in animation were affected just as hard as men. A handful of women would remain at the studio and help Disney confront the challenges that lay in front of them. Nathalia Holt's book *The Queens of Animation* explores the work of female animators at Disney over time in great detail. She draws attention to a handful of women who would have a big impact on the look of Disney films.

In the aftermath of the war, a group of women who had been promoted while the men were away were reluctant to let go of their roles. Women like Katherine Kerwin, Ruthie Thompson, Mimi Thorton, and Thelma Witmer played a vital role in shaping the movies that Disney brought to the screen in the immediate postwar era. Their contributions to some of Disney's best-known movies, such as *Cinderella*, *Alice in Wonderland*, and *Peter Pan*, included the creation of perspective in many scenes in *Alice*, as well as bringing the fluttering sparkle to Tinker Bell. Disney Studios, like many other employers of the day, valued women less than men to the point of paying them less even when they were doing similar work. The company's most trusted senior animators were known as Disney's Nine Old Men. Hired early on, many controlled much of the work the studio did. As the nickname indicates, every last one was a man.

All this came to a head with the release of *Sleeping Beauty*, featuring the work of many female animators at Disney. *Sleeping Beauty* was significant to the studio and their workers in many ways. Released in January 1959, the movie was a six-year effort. Women had taken many jobs related to the production of the movie. Unfortunately, while the film cost over $6 million, it yielded only a little over $5 million in ticket sales.

The Shaggy Dog was the studio's first live-action comedy film. It only cost $1 million to make, and became a big hit, with over 8 million in sales by the end of the year. Over the next year, Disney Studios dramatically downsized the studio's art animated art department. They were able to do this in part because of the Xerox machine. Xerography led to lower-quality animation, but it was also a lot faster and cheaper than the hand-painted cels that animators had originally used to create Disney films.

The results were devastating for many women who worked as Disney's artists. As Nathalia Holt recounts, "Ink and Paint, the division that hired more women than any other, was slowly being stripped clean." Disney's next feature and the first to use this process was *One Hundred and One Dalmatians*. Once again, even though a number of women worked on that film, only two were acknowledged at all when the credits rolled.

Of all the women who Walt Disney worked with over the course of his career, one stood out. Mary Blair worked on many projects directly under the supervision of Walt Disney. She helped tell the color story for films such as *Cinderella* and *Peter Pan*. Blair was also one of the few female artists whom Walt respected as an artist in her own right. Her work drew inspiration from many places, including homemade quilts. After touring South America with Walt Disney, her modernist imagery would have a place in the company's work for over two decades. When Disney wanted a design for the It's a Small World After All ride, it was to Blair that he looked. She was one of the few artists whom he allowed to work as a freelancer from her home in Long Island.

Others were not as lucky. After Disney's death, women may have been entering the workforce in greater numbers at other companies, but not at Disney. Only a tenth of the studio's employees were women. Women were only allowed to be assistant animators rather than being given a chance to assume a leading role. After the studio began making high-quality animated movies again in the 1990s, women began slowly filling the ranks of the studio's animators and directors. Roughly one in three women worked in the studio's animation division. Women like Ellen Woodbury, Linda Woolverton, Rita Hsaio, and Brenda Chapman have taken over where pioneers like Mary Blair, Retta Scott, and Bianca Majoli had originally led. Scott and Majoli had been recruited in part to work on *Bambi*. During their short time at the studio, each would have an impact on the look of several Disney classics.

As *Frozen* came to life, what had once been only a handful of women in the animation field became over a dozen. The promotion of women in the animation field that Walt Disney had managed in part is likely to continue as the studio continues to look for talent wherever they can find it. As more and more women join Disney's ranks, they are also likely to continue to stretch the company's work in new directions. Princesses may be what the company is best known for, but female animators are finding other places to show girls exactly what they can be as young women and long after they grow up. Marriage is no longer the only possibility for the female lead. Her happily ever after is there for her to make all her own.

Was Disney Anti-Semitic?

The dictionary definition of the word "anti-Semitism" is "hostility to, prejudice, or discrimination against Jews." Hatred of Jews is an ancient prejudice, one of the world's oldest forms of bigotry. Europe was a particular hotbed of hatred, religious intolerance, and pogroms long before the Holocaust. Many Jews chose to emigrate to the United States during the second great wave of American migration from 1880–1924. They sought to escape European societal restrictions that confined them to ghettos. Jewish culture began to have an impact not only on the places in America where Jews primarily settled, such as New York City, but also other parts of the country.

One area of American life that Jews made their own was the entertainment industry. Works such as *Hollywood's Chosen People: The Jewish Experience in American Cinema* by editors Daniel Bernardi, Murray Pomerance, and Hava Tirosh-Samuelson, and *An Empire of Their Own: How the Jews Invented Hollywood* by Neal Gabler, chart the vast influence of American Jews on the world of Hollywood and how such influence changed the very nature of the nascent industry. As the authors of *Hollywood's Chosen People* relate:

> Within three decades after the mass migration of the 1880s, Jews were enjoying unprecedented material ease and, according to Eric Goldstein, the Jewish working class had largely vanished. Jews entered the motion picture industry in droves—an industry revitalized by the conversion to sound (by 1932) and closely allied with the garment industry (because of the link between motion pictures and costume design and a common system of labor practices [Toll]). During the 1910s and 1920s, as studios were springing up in Southern California, Los Angeles emerged as the nation's fourth-largest city and became a major Jewish center. The original Hollywood moguls included men like Jack and Sam Warner, who had been in the entertainment business in Ohio, and Sam Goldwyn, who had partnered with Adolph Zukor and Jesse Lasky in New York. The movie business and the Jewish experience came to share the Hollywood sun.

Actors, directors, and studio executives changed their names to sound less Jewish. They did this while still retaining a culturally Jewish outlook and a sense of being part of the Jewish community. Many Jews in the entertainment industry had a complicated relationship with Judaism. Members of the movie industry on one hand embraced intermarriage and discarded Jewish traditions such as keeping kosher. On the other hand, they also found a sense of kin and closeness with their fellow Jews, however tenuous. Hollywood tends to be a very insular place, where outsiders are kept at bay. Jews were also up against the same classic prejudice in many parts of the United States that they faced in other parts of the world. Anti-Semitism was a particular issue in the United States in the 1920s and 1930s. Nationally renowned and influential anti-Semitic figures like Father Charles Coughlin and Charles Lindbergh argued in the late 1930s that Jews were a third column bent on pulling the United States toward Communism and another world war.

Walt Disney created a place of his own in Hollywood. After his first incredible success with *Steamboat Willie*, Disney was no longer an outsider. He was very much part of the Hollywood establishment. He may have been viewed as a dreamer with utterly unrealistic expectations for animation, but he was also someone making money in the movie business and earning many awards in the process. As part of his work in Hollywood, Disney worked with many Jewish people. Over time, Walt Disney has developed a reputation as an anti-Semite who actively and directly hated Jews. Historians and those who love Disney have examined the issue and come to some essential conclusions.

Was Disney an anti-Semite? A close reading of his work and life can only lead to a definitive no. Like many other aspects of his work and his personal life, the answer to this question is complicated by contemporary perceptions as well as his own actions. Author Neal Gabler is one of Disney's most important biographers, and certainly the person who has had the chance to view all that Disney did, from the beginning to the end of his life. In writing about this immensely comprehensive work on Disney, *Walt Disney: The Triumph of the American Imagination,* Gabler reminds his readers that he read all of Disney's papers in the archives. He writes, "Though Walt himself, in my estimation, was not anti-Semitic, nevertheless, he willingly allied himself with people who were anti-Semitic, and that reputation stuck. He was never really able to expunge it throughout his life." At the same time, Gabler also states outright, "I saw no evidence, other than casual anti-Semitism that virtually every gentile at that time would have, that Walt Disney was an anti-Semite."

What the notion of casual anti-Semitism actually means, and how this had an impact on the company's work, have become subjects worthy of thoughtful consideration and careful examination. The treatment of Jews in the United States is an example of the way that Americans were changing as the American population expanded and grew. In the aftermath of the Holocaust, anti-Semitism is arguably no longer tolerated, at least in most circles in the United States. This was not true, either in public or in private, for much of Disney's life. Many of his lauded contemporaries were anti-Semitic in some way. By the mid-1920s, over 4 million Americans had joined the Ku Klux Klan. In that same era, millionaire industrialist Henry Ford actively promoted hatred of Jews. Ford used his own media outlets, such as the *Dearborn Independent* newspaper, to argue that an enormous, deliberate Jewish conspiracy was ruining the United States.

Walt Disney did not share the views of his near-contemporaries. He hired many Jews to work at his studio and freely promoted them without prejudice. He donated money to Jewish charities. His local chapter of B'nai B'rith, an organization dedicated to protecting Jews from discrimination, made him their Man of the Year in 1958. Disney gave Nazi propagandist Leni Riefenstahl a tour of the studio in 1938, but he also deliberately walked away from her work a short time later. In 1941, many Disney animators went on strike. A few were Jewish and argued that Disney did not hire them again based on their Jewish background. However, Disney in part operated as part of a cult of personality. Many studio actions centered on him and his viewpoints. This was his place, and people wanted his approval. They needed it to advance in his company and earn the ability to engage in creative work. Disney was extremely upset about the strike. After it ended, he refused to hire many people because they had been part of the strike rather than because they were Jewish.

Walt Disney can occasionally be accused of including characters in his work that fit the definition of classic anti-Semitic depictions of Jews. In the 1933 animated short *The Three Little Pigs*, for instance, the Big Bad Wolf takes the role of a demeaning Jewish peddler, out to cheat his clients, much to the disgust of the American Jewish Congress. Disney didn't address their complaints about the film until many years later. His later works, however, are largely devoid of such stereotypes against Jews. He also demanded six-day workweeks from his employees, including mandatory Saturday overtime, during the height of massive productions like *Snow White*.

Writers who have examined Disney's body of work closely tend to agree with Douglas Brode, the Jewish author of *Multiculturalism and the Mouse: Race and Sex in Disney Entertainment*. He states, "There is zero hard evidence that Disney ever wrote or said anything anti-Semitic in private or public. His films feature a wide array of great Jewish actors in the most diverse roles imaginable, more so than any other studio of Hollywood's golden age, including those run by Jewish movie moguls. Finally, there is no evidence in the work of anti-Semitism via negatively portrayed Jewish characters."

In later years, Disney allied himself with an organization called the Motion Picture Alliance for the Preservation of American Ideals (MPA).

Formed in 1944, the primary goal of the MPA was to convince a group of Hollywood insiders to testify before Congress that the film industry included many Communist sympathizers. MPA members were largely white, conservative, and Protestant. They saw themselves as holding up the ideals of the United States during a time of great upheaval and dangerous war. In response, Hollywood's more liberal members would go on to form the Council of Hollywood Guilds and Unions. Many members of the council were Jewish, as were a few MPA members. The council charged the MPA with stifling the community's creativity, a view shared by many Americans. Walt Disney and many founding members of the MPA eventually left the organization and disavowed its goals.

Perhaps the most intriguing thing about the question of whether Walt Disney was anti-Semitic is that the answer ultimately doesn't seem to matter to many people. Disney hired and promoted very obviously Jewish people like Kay Kamen very early in his career. He contributed to Jewish charities and gave little evidence of engaging in the kind of bigotry that Henry Ford relished. The perception that he was anti-Semitic lingers in the world's collective memory, even though historians have found little evidence to back it up. Like much of his life and work, the myths surrounding Walt Disney are, in many ways, far more fascinating than the authentic truth.

Racism in Disney's World: The Enduring Legacy of *Song of the South*

Biographies of Walt Disney and his company must be prepared to address more than the impact that Disney had on the world. An examination of his work and the history of the company must also focus on how it might have made a difference in the world but did not. Of all the many criticisms that can be leveled against Walt Disney and the studio as a whole, there are several that stick out. Disney and his executives had an undeniably paternalistic view of women. In his films, women are there largely to serve as prizes for men. He occasionally promoted women in his studio, but he also kept them out of the more powerful roles and often failed to give them artistic credit. Disney has been accused of anti-Semitism but, despite popular beliefs to the contrary, this charge has little factual evidence.

When viewed through the inevitable lens of history and innate principles of essential social justice, Walt and the people he promoted, worked with, and trusted were very much a product of their time. Their views were often fundamentally antediluvian, and occasionally deeply disturbing. Disney repeatedly came under well-deserved fire for his company's dogged determination to cling to the worst American societal flaws. This can be seen in his depictions of the role of African Americans and others who did not fit the role of the standard American that the company made the norm in his entertainment outlets. During his lifetime, the majority of Americans were white, and they expected the culture to reflect this in their entertainment choices. In Disney's animation shorts, full-length movies, and even in his theme parks, racism was both unconsciously and consciously very much part of the background. Active racism occasionally, sadly, and deliberately was part of Disney's narrative. Rather than challenging this form of stereotyping in American society, Disney was part of efforts to reinforce prevailing systems of oppression and reduce Blacks to simple and insulting clichés. The same can be said about his depictions of many other non-whites. Using easy, lazy, and often vaguely offensive ways to show other cultures continued well after his death. Efforts to address such problems are an ongoing and evolving source of debate in the company today.

Racism in films is as old as filmmaking itself. Released in 1915, the silent film *Birth of a Nation* is an iconic, historic milestone with brutally racist imagery. Pulitzer Prize–winning film critic Roger Ebert draws attention to the techniques that the director, D. W. Griffiths, invented: "He did not create the language of cinema so much as codify and demonstrate it, so that after him it became conventional for directors to tell a scene by cutting between wide (or 'establishing') shots and various medium shots, close-ups, and inserts of details." At the same time, as Ebert and many others have remarked, the film also drips with bigotry. *Birth of a Nation* is all about racism. African American men are shown as little more than as sexually violent predators that the KKK must fight in order to protect white women.

Practices that this notorious film popularized would plague the industry for decades. Rather than use Black actors in roles calling for African Americans, we saw actors in blackface instead. The film deliberately misrepresented American and world history and turned to stereotypes in lieu of well-thought-out, complicated characters. Griffith set the tone for the film industry's depiction of Blacks and Black culture over the decades that followed. His work was incredibly influential for many decades and made the movie industry another facet of oppression rather than artistic liberation. At best, Walt Disney, like many of his contemporaries in the entertainment field, was carelessly oblivious to the racism that he was conveying to his audiences. At worst, he was an active participant in the process of promoting racist imagery.

Examples of nonchalant stereotyping can be readily found in many Disney works. In *Peter Pan*, released in 1953, Indigenous people are called "redskins," an ethnic slur of long standing. Disney officials would later describe the section where Peter and the Lost Boys don native headdresses and dance as a "form of mockery and appropriation of Native peoples' culture and imagery." People are not the only characters who behave poorly in Disney films. In *Lady and the Tramp*, Disney's 1955 film, Si and Am are evil Siamese cats who sing "The Siamese Cat Song" in broken English. In a 2019 remake, Si and Am are replaced by Devon Rex cats, who sing a jazz number called "What a Shame." A second racist depiction of Asians via yet another Siamese cat character can be seen in *The Aristocats* in 1970. Shun Gon sings another racist song in broken English, with demeaning references to Chinese culture, while he plays the piano with chopsticks.

Of all the problems with racism in Disney films, it was in his work with African Americans where Disney and the company failed most spectacularly. Overt racism can be seen in many Disney films. In the original 1940 version of *Fantasia*, for example, the centaurs in the "Pastoral Symphony" segment include a young, Black female centaur dubbed Sunflower—the first African American character in Disney's feature films. Unfortuntely, she is no more than an ugly caricature. Sunflower has exaggerated lips and a hairstyle that mocks traditional African American hairstyles. She's there solely to serve the other centaurs. Her character was considered so offensive that the entire sequence was cut from the second release of the film in 1969 and all future releases. While working on *Fantasia*, the animators worked with Hattie Noel, a Black performer who would go on to play many roles in Hollywood in the 1940s. The actress was made to wear a form-fitting ballet leotard that did not flatter her body type. Adding insult to injury, Disney's animators mocked Noel as they watched her dance. Her body served as the model for the dancing hippo sequence in a role meant to equate Black women's bodies with jungle animals. *Dumbo* is taught how to fly by a group of crows with Black voices that use highly stereotyped language. King Louie in *The Jungle Book* was widely criticized for depicting African Americans as lazy and lacking in linguistic abilities when first brought to the screen in 1968.

In 1946, Disney went a step further. *Song of the South* combines live action and animation. Disney would return to this technique again and again, in part because live action was so much cheaper than full-length animation. The film is based on the writings of Joel Chandler Harris and his Black Uncle Remus character. Harris was a white journalist who popularized African American folktales he heard while living on a plantation in the pre–Civil War era in the 1880s. Like many Americans (including Mark Twain), Disney read and remembered them as he grew up. In

Disney's version of the story, a young white boy runs away from his home and happens upon Uncle Remus singing. Remus tells young Johnny tales about crafty wildlife creatures and their adventures.

On the surface, the movie seems to be the kind of tale that Disney specialized in: an older character telling stories to a young audience. A closer examination reveals layers of offensive stereotypes that Disney deliberately chooses to bring to the screen.

The setting of the movie appears to be uncertain. Viewers are left wondering if the characters are slaves or free people. Worse, the overarching theme is that Blacks were content, even happy, to be slaves and unhappy at being set free. Even more than in many movies of the era, the dialogue used by the African American characters is enmeshed with language meant to convey the second-class status of Blacks and the implication that they were delighted with this arrangement. Black Uncle Remus tips his hat to the white character Miss Doshy, who owns the plantation. As they go about menial tasks such as working in the cotton fields, the African American characters sing upbeat songs. Remus is the "venerable old darkey" who conveys wisdom while still being a figure of contempt for the white characters. Unlike the other white adult characters in the movie, he lacks grace and power. Audiences are left with the impression that freeing the slaves was a foolish mistake. Everyone should simply accept the status quo, the film implies, even when it is a great moral evil.

Ironically, the film went through several versions before Disney made it in an attempt to expunge the offensive material. The original screenplay by Dalton Redmond was "allegedly full of racial bias," according to author Nathalia Holt. Jewish screenwriter Maurice Rapf, who would later be blackballed from the movie industry due to his refusal to testify before the House Un-American Activities Committee (HUAC), worked on the film treatment with Redmond. He told Disney that he thought the project was a mistake that would make the studio look bad. Disney said to him, "That's why I want someone like you to work on it. You're against the black stereotypes. Most of us, even if we have no racial bias, commit boo-boos that offend people all of the time. Because you are sensitive to the problem, maybe you can avoid it." Rapf repeatedly tried to remove some of the more pejorative terms. He tried to make it clear that the movie was set in the post–Civil War era so the characters were not pleased about being so servile. Redmond was furious at these changes. Rapf walked away and allowed Redmond to claim full credit for the entire screenplay, even as his name remained in the final credits.

Many African American leaders wanted Disney to drop the project because of the obvious racism of the Uncle Remus stories. When the film was released, it was universally condemned by many community leaders. According to published reports in the *New York Times*, protestors carried signs in front of the theaters where it was shown, with taglines such as, "We fought for Uncle Sam, not Uncle Tom." Congressman Adam Clayton Powell Jr. called the film "an insult to American minorities." Even *New York Times* critic Bosley Crowther wrote to Disney to condemn it for arguing that the "master-and-slave relation is so lovingly regarded in your yarn with the Negroes bowing and scraping and singing spirituals in the night, that one might almost imagine that you figure Abe Lincoln made a mistake. Put down that mint julep, Mr. Disney!"

Song of the South won an Oscar for Best Song for "Zip-a-Dee-Doo-Dah" and made a small profit to boot. For those examining this issue at a distance, the question becomes why Disney allowed the project to go forward at all. Why did he ignore the useful advice that he was given by many respected industry insiders, as well as members of the African American community? Intense criticism from contemporaries like Crowther make it hard for Disney to argue that he was just demonstrating how things were during this period. Critics have pointed to the supposed resemblance of Uncle Remus and Disney himself, in that both were telling stories to young children. But as in many other areas of his life, Disney was ultimately on a path and would not be deterred from it. The kind of personal determination that led him to create movie classics such as *Snow White* and *Pinocchio* also led to his refusal to abandon a project that he must have realized would ultimately reflect badly on him and his studio.

The film was re-released in theaters as late as 1986. However, unlike other Oscar-winning movies, it has not been given an official Disney video release. No video is available for the home audience. People can find pirated copies overseas. Film historians and those who are simply curious can also find many scenes from the movie on YouTube. Disney Studios made a conscious decision not to release *Song of the South* on either the Disney Channel or Disney+. In a meeting with shareholders in 2010, Disney chief executive officer (CEO) Bob Iger described the film as "fairly offensive."

The company has dealt with the issue of racism in its other films by putting up a disclaimer after realizing some of the studio's most prized works have issues with race that cannot be ignored. In 2019, viewers on Disney+ were warned about some of the company's classic works with a brief statement applied to some of the movies and cartoons. "This program is presented as originally created. It may contain outdated cultural depictions," read one label. In 2020, Disney went a step further. Before certain titles are shown, viewers are given a warning intended to illustrate that the company is well aware of the racial issues that plagued part of the company's work. Disney+ viewers see a message stating, "This program includes negative depictions and/or mistreatment of people or cultures. These stereotypes were wrong then and are wrong now. Rather than remove this content, we want to acknowledge its harmful impact, learn from it, and spark conversation to create a more inclusive future together."

Despite *Song of the South*'s undeniably racist history, the company created a ride in 1989 called Splash Mountain for Disneyland, Disney World, and Tokyo Disney. Splash Mountain takes passengers through scenes from the movie as they follow the adventures of Br'er Rabbit. In 2020, Disney officials finally responded to ongoing criticism of the use of the film in their theme parks. The *Song of the South* scenes have been replaced by scenes from 2009's *The Princess and the Frog*. While the film features the company's first Black princess, the main character suffers from the baleful polymorph trope, in which people are turned into animals or helpless fictional creatures. Tiana has no agency of her own. Critics are left to wonder if Disney really has changed, and when (or even whether) further changes will take place.

In leaving the movie in the vaults, some African Americans leaders and entertainers such as Whoopi Goldberg have argued that Disney is doing its fans an injustice in the long run. Rather than ban the film completely, it might be better to examine it in greater detail and use scenes and dialogue to further our understanding about all sorts of biases that people may not be aware of when they watch any form of entertainment. As Goldberg states in an interview with Nathalia Holt, this way, "we can talk about what it was and where it came from and why it came out." Goldberg has long spoken out about this issue and how to respond to degrading imagery.

Disney is not the only company to grapple with the issue of racism in old films and cartoons. Vintage cartoons from Warner Bros. are dotted with problematic representations. Blackface is seen frequently in their cartoons, as well as simplistic depictions of African Americans. In 2013, Goldberg was enlisted to speak on behalf of Warner Bros. She provided a detailed statement about the studio's *Tom and Jerry* cartoons and how audiences should respond in the face of disturbing racial and ethnic portrayals. She tells her viewers, "These prejudices were wrong then and they're wrong today," but she also believes that they should be seen by modern audiences. Watching even the most disturbing imagery may be the best way to have a fuller understanding of the impact that such depictions have had on American culture and the way that Disney—the man and the company—did little to confront or change American racism.

The Great Walt Disney Cartoonists Strike of 1941 and Its Aftermath: Working Conditions at Disney

Walt Disney came from a remarkably humble background. His blue-collar heritage was authentic and would remain so all his life. The young man who got up before dawn to deliver papers and help put food on his family's table knew what it was like to work extremely long hours for scant pay. This might have given Disney an understanding that hard work should be amply compensated once he took on the role of supervisor, but it did not. Working conditions at the company's studios and parks have a long and dishonorable history. People bent over cels drawing for hours were largely given neither financial reward nor the emotional compensation of seeing their names on the finished product. Park workers are asked to smile constantly and put on a false front while enduring intense heat and repetitive tasks. Disney executives have been at best indifferent to the plight of their employees and too often willing to take profits while failing to offer adequate compensation to the people they entrusted with carrying out the company's fundamental ideals.

In many ways, the problems that studio workers faced began with Disney's lack of training in business techniques and his ambivalence about his role in the company. Unlike many of today's corporate executives, Walt Disney was not an Ivy Leaguer, nor was he trained in the field of business. Like many of his contemporaries, he wasn't even a high school graduate. This gave him much in common with the people he worked with. Later in life, Disney would receive many honorary degrees. Harvard's president called him a magician, and Yale and the University of Southern California (USC) also gave him praise and credentials. Despite these awards, Disney remained aware of his background and educational personal shortcomings. In movies like *Fantasia*, we can see how he yearned to demonstrate an ability to show his mastery of classical music and other things people associated with an upper-class upbringing.

Disney was caught between two worlds. On one hand, he wanted to be a benevolent, rich patron of the arts. He was also a driven person with an innate vision. On the other hand, he was beholden to his shareholders and the bankers who financed his movies. The people who did the honest hard work of creating his plans were often caught in the middle.

Disney did not necessarily seek to get rich from his work. Most of the profits from the most successful movies were often plowed right back into his next project. He did, however, freely and happily enjoy the fruits of his labor. He had a nice house and new cars, and he took many trips to Europe. America's Uncle Walt came to work in a chauffeur-driven limousine. The same was true for his brother Roy, who also enjoyed a great many perks and retired a very rich man, leaving a huge estate to his grandchildren. When he died, Walt was worth over $100 million in 1966 dollars.

The contemporary Walt Disney Company has assets in the billions, making it one of the world's richest entertainment companies. Over the years, despite the fact that Disney has made a great deal of money, company officials have been repeatedly (and deservedly) accused of not sharing the wealth with their workers. Many executives have been incredibly greedy. In 1993, Michael Eisner lined his pockets with two-thirds of the company's yearly profits. Other executives have taken millions of dollars in salary, even when the company's stock tanks. The contentious issue of who should profit from Disney's work continues to divide top management and ever so slightly stain the company's reputation.

Disney's workers have not been given the same access to the company's earnings. In 2019, as political science professor Peter Dreier points out in an article in *The Nation* entitled, "Disney Is Not the Greatest Place on Earth to Work," "Disney earned $14 billion in profits and the company's board gave Iger an 80 percent boost in his compensation to $65.7 million. His annual compensation was 1,424 times what the median Disney worker earned—one of the widest CEO-worker gaps of any American corporation." Disney's great-niece, Abigail Disney, has castigated the company's policies for being unfair to its employees.

The company's record when it comes to its treatment of workers is decidedly mixed at best. Disney's first animation company declared bankruptcy. *Steamboat Willie*, his greatest early success, was released in late 1928, a year before the Great Depression. After the stock market crashed, American unemployment climbed as high as 25 percent. Disney was one of the few companies hiring rather than firing people. Workers seeking positions from artists to secretaries sent in stacks of résumés each day in the hope of getting a job. Applicants saw a hugely successful company putting out imaginative products that the world wanted.

However, the reality was not as easy or as pleasant as the image. Employees often worked long hours for comparatively low wages. As explained earlier in this chapter, women in particular were expected to put in a lot of effort, while not earning a good salary, or even on-screen credit. Many men labored under the same conditions. Instead of the promised bonuses after *Snow White* was finished, workers were laid off. Despite the fact that Disney wanted to create his own workers' paradise with a beautiful campus, company workers were asked to put in incredibly long hours, with few breaks.

Matters came to a head in what author, Disney animator, and former president of the Animation Guild Local 839 Tom Sito called the "Great Walt Disney Cartoonists Strike of 1941." The strike would have a vast impact not only on Disney, but also on the animation industry as a whole. Fierce allegations were made against the company in the media. Friendships were broken up. Artists who had been an integral part of the studio left, and new faces took their place. Part of the essential problem was that while the studio had grown to over 1,200 employees, it was still run as one man's fiefdom. Disney was not a professional businessperson with a master's of business administration (MBA). Raises were handed out seemingly at random. He also tended to treat employees with a certain ruthless indifference. When his own sister-in-law, Hazel, suffered a nervous breakdown, he reduced her paycheck when she missed work. He did not understand, or refused to admit, that workers wanted a fair salary and decent working conditions instead of a benevolent patriarchy.

After Disney's first flush of incredible financial and critical success with *Snow White*, the next two movies, *Pinocchio* and *Fantasia*, failed miserably, financially if not critically. Disney was not sure how to respond. Workers at the company, while lamenting the difficult conditions, were also unsure if they were a group of elite artists or more akin to factory workers on an assembly line. Animators ultimately decided that they needed a union. Complicated negotiations and attempts at union organizing continued for years.

Disney did not want a union at his company. Under the Franklin D. Roosevelt administration, legislation such as the National Labor Relations Act of 1935 gave workers rights that included the right to unionize, demand collective bargaining, and strike if their demands were not met. When animator Art Babbitt, known for his creation of Goofy and 13 other characters, asked for a union, Disney would have none of it. He ignored the legal requirements of the law and fired Babbitt and his fellow animators on May 29, 1941. The next day, over 300 Disney workers went on strike.

Many Disney employees were conflicted about their decision to strike. World War II was in full progress in Europe, cutting off a source of revenue for the studio. Animators wanted to continue making *Dumbo,* as they knew that without it, the studio might lose audiences and revenues. Jobs continued to be scarce, especially in the entertainment industry. At the same time, workers were frustrated with arbitrary raises and issues such as mandatory Saturday working hours. Disney saw the strike as a personal affront rather than a demand for a well-earned share of the profits that came from hours spent hunched over wielding tiny brushes and dealing with a demanding, often capricious boss.

For the next nine weeks, Disney and many employees had to pass through their fellow workers to get to work. Strikers held up hand-drawn signs mocking Disney's work with the characters that the animators had helped create. "LEONARDO, MICHELANGELO, and TITIAN WERE UNION MEN," read one. Another had a drawing of Pluto under the message, "I'D RATHER BE A DOG THAN A SCAB!" Five weeks after the strike started, Walt left the country to tour South America with a few handpicked personal favorite staffers in tow. In the end, Disney blinked. By mid-September, the strike was over. Disney unionized, and the workers won the right to overtime pay.

Walt Disney never forgot or forgave the workers who struck. They were the first to be fired when cutbacks came, and they were often overlooked when it came to promotions. When Disney testified in front of HUAC, he argued that Communists had been behind the strike. He would later argue that the strike had been a boon to him, as it allowed him to fire people who were not willing to carry out his vision in every detail. Some of the workers who did leave went on to play a major role in other animated features made by other studios. Disney's art director, Maurice Noble, headed for Warner Bros., where he contributed to the studio's distinctively surreal style. Bill Melendez would go on to direct the beloved children's classic *A Charlie Brown Christmas* and other Peanuts animated features.

The 1941 strike, while affecting the more than 1,200 workers at Disney at the time, had a lasting effect on a company that has grown to over 200,000 workers today. During Walt Disney's lifetime, Disney's employees continued to struggle with the idiosyncratic head of the company and his changing management style. Creativity mattered to him, but the growing burden of managing many projects at the same time often drove him to inefficiency and lack of control at the company.

Over the next two decades, Disney took on an organizational structure that did little to sort out the company's internal chain of command or allow enough delegation. In the late 1940s, he and many of his employees felt adrift. The energy that had pushed them to create masterpieces of animation dissipated in the aftermath of the war. Other animation studios were taking over, putting a new spin on and bringing new energy to the art that Disney did not match. Disney Studios had held the reins in the industry for over a decade. This was due in large part to its reputation as a place where talent was recognized and rewarded, as well as the chance that it offered talented artists to be part of cutting-edge projects. When the strike made clear that this was not always the case, some of the company's creative energy (along with its workers) went to other animation studios. Workers no longer felt the same sense that they were making history when they had worked on productions like *Snow White* or *Pinocchio*. While they continued to churn out animated films like *Cinderella* that caught the public's attention and adulation, the studio did not occupy the central place that it had had before the war. Disney turned much of his attention to his plans for Disneyland instead of filmmaking. Disneyland took up all his creative energy during the last decades of his life. The amusement park would come to embody much of the disdain that he often felt for some of his employees and the human toll that it took to bring his ideas to life.

Disney famously said, "You can dream, create, design, and build the most wonderful place in the world . . . but it requires people to make the dream a reality." Disney workers continue to push the company to live up to the ideals Disney set up when it was first founded. Disneyland is supposed to be "The Happiest Place on Earth." Staffers at the parks are required to adhere to a dress code that includes everything from having no visible tattoos to the type of underwear they can wear. Before meeting with the public, workers must undergo training in the company ethos, including hours of watching the company's films and talking about Walt Disney's original plans. Even the nomenclature is distinctive: visitors are "guests," and employees are called "cast members."

The essential goal of Disney's amusement parks is to provide a place where people can relax and have a great time. Unfortunately the people who make his dream a reality continue to be undervalued and underpaid. Even when working for hours in high heat and humidity and cumbersome costumes, they are expected to be clean, neat, and cheerful. Over the years, the company has held its workers to high standards, while not always living up to such standards for itself when it comes to pay and working conditions. The company has taken a great deal of heat over employee policies that have often fobbed the real costs of labor off on taxpayers and the local community.

A list of ways in which the company has failed to adhere to the highest ethical standards for their employees is long and varied. Over the years, workers have staged several strikes at Disney parks, including Disneyland, Disney World, and Disneyland Paris, because of low pay and lack of wage increases. Workers abroad have also been affected. Toys, clothing, and other items sold in the parks and stores came under scrutiny after a report by the National Labor Committee found workers toiling for pennies an hour in overseas sweatshops to produce the goods. Similar conditions at home led to settled lawsuits in Florida and California. Workers have faced issues ranging from Disney's refusal to shoulder their healthcare costs to the company's demand for temp workers rather than paying for salaried posts.

Workplace safety has also been an ongoing issue. Several Disney workers have been killed on the job from events such as a monorail crash and ride accidents. The company has also come under fire for other practices, such as requiring workers to train new workers to do their jobs so they could outsource their positions to lower-paid immigrant workers. In a scathing 2017 survey of Disney workers, many reported serious personal problems that included food insecurity, childcare problems, changing schedules, lack of affordable healthcare access, below-average wages, and even homelessness. This went on even as the company reported enormous profits and an increase in the cost of their parks' tickets.

Workers have also been reliant on state welfare just to make ends meet. Meanwhile, "a *Los Angeles Times* investigation from 2017 found that the company had secured rebates and other incentives from the city worth more than $1 billion." The rise of COVID-19 has created further labor issues for company officials and workers. Workers have alleged that the company has not taken sufficient precautions to ensure worker and visitor safety as a result of the coronavirus. Layoffs in the aftermath of the appearance of the virus have created further disruptions for workers, as parks have been open with either limited capacity or shuttered completely.

When Disneyland first opened, Walt Disney said, "Disneyland is dedicated to the ideals, the dreams, and the hard facts that have created America." Disney's historically combative view of labor relations illustrates the many struggles that American workers have long faced when finding their own personal American dream. His failure to hear what his workers had to say about the on-the-job conditions they faced was tone deaf at best. As representatives of American values to the rest of the world, Disney executives might have made a difference by standing up for American workers and their right to a decent salary for a day's work. Instead, those who run the company have been all too willing to make demands on workers without providing adequate compensation or a supportive and safe working environment.

CHAPTER SIX

An Empire of Imagination: New Directions for Disney

In examining Walt Disney's work and the impact of his company on the world in the aftermath of his death, change is one of the single most important underlying driving forces. A willingness to challenge how things are done is a hallmark of the company's overall history. After his first startling success, Disney and his studio were frequently under pressure to produce as many new animation films as possible and come up with brand-new ideas for his fans. Capturing the audience's attention and keeping it was the only way to keep the studio afloat financially.

For most of his life, his work and the work of his employees was marked by a series of projects with tight deadlines and soaring expectations. *Steamboat Willie* was a landmark in animation, but it was not enough to create a lasting career. Disney wanted something even bigger. *Snow White and the Seven Dwarfs* followed after years of experimentation and almost breathtaking artistic risks. In the next decade, the studio brought out a series of original, beautifully realized animated films that pushed the boundaries of the art and created the foundations of the field of American animated movies. Under Disney's leadership, his company also happily embraced many types of new technology. The silent films of his early career gave way to employing sound and synchronizing it with visual images to tell a story. Then it was on to the use of vivid color and the creation of a series of new and deeply appealing characters. Disney looked to fairy tales for ideas and then brought them to contemporary viewers with movies designed to please both children and adults. Other Hollywood studios dismissed television as no more than a temporary fad. Disney saw the medium as a way to reach even greater audiences for his films, his parks, and his original programming. He revived the old-fashioned amusement park and updated it for the modern world. His successors have gone in new directions in animation that have reinvigorated the field yet again. The post–Walt Disney works of the 1990s include many lovely, ingenious films that can be happily added to the Disney canon and the list of classic American art. Disney officials have added to the company's holdings with other film studios and amusement parks on several continents.

The process of exploring and bringing new ideas to life continues to be a major part of the work that the company does as its officials look to the future of the industry. Fans who grew up watching Disney movies want to bring their children to Disney amusement parks and teach them to appreciate the beauty of the exquisitely rendered scenes in *Bambi*, *Cinderella*, and (later) *Toy Story* and *Up*. Disney parks continue to draw in crowds of all ages. Children come with their parents to enjoy old favorites like the teacup ride at Disneyland and transfer fun childhood memories to the next generation. The word "Disney" means something special to every generation of American children.

At the same time, fans also expect entirely new rides, new concepts, and new films at the box office from the company each year. Fans have also come to expect that Disney officials will look to explore the darker side of the company and grapple with issues posed by some of its less-than-stellar works. The open racism of *Song of the South* has been replaced in Splash Mountain by scenes featuring an African American Disney princess. Anti-Asian stereotypes in Disney movies have also been replaced by the company's commitment to respecting other cultures in spaces like Shanghai Disney. Working closely with China's authoritarian government must be balanced with the ideal of respecting democratic protest.

Company officials realize that they must be mindful of varied points of view as they present new media for public consumption. Critics hold studio officials to higher standards of inclusion than they did in the past. In turn, those who run the company are still trying to figure out what it means to be both an American company and a presence on the global stage. That may be the fundamental question that the company must answer as it continues to occupy a unique niche in the entertainment world.

A Shining City on a Hill or a Conformist Paradise? Creating Epcot

Epcot is one of the most American of all acronyms. These five letters occupy a unique place in the American psyche, like NASA or the FBI. For Walt Disney, Epcot was not just another offhand concept. Rather, the park was meant to be the embodiment of a certain ideal that was as central to his vision of humanity as his movies and theme parks. Today, the

Experimental Prototype Community of Tomorrow is not the kind of community that Disney wanted—it's just another part of Disney World. Visitors can explore the supposed future that Disney officials see in the form of new rides in one area and then head off to learn about 11 countries in another part of the park. As an amusement park, Epcot is well worth a whole day of exploration. Clever rides, great shows, superb food, and a stunning evening fireworks show have brought in many repeat visitors.

But the park is also hindered by the lack of a grounding theme that brings it all together in the public mind. Unlike other Disney parks like Animal Kingdom, where the audience knows what's going to happen, Epcot does not quite entirely come together as a whole. It's a mishmash of what feel like leftover Disney ideas instead of being a fully realized space. That's in part because Epcot wasn't originally intended to be an amusement venue. Instead of another place designed around mere amusement, it was supposed to be where Walt Disney could realize some of his personal ideals and serve as a source of inspiration for the company's architects, workers, and management. This was going to be his shining city on a hill, where he could illustrate both a radical transformation of existing American life and a return to what he saw as America's historic, intrinsic goodness. Like many other attempts at a planned utopian community, it never came to full fruition.

Even as he was forever talking about his love of farming and tiny towns, Walt spent most of his life as a city and suburban dweller. The only time he lived in a really small town was during his childhood years in Marceline. And yet, despite his choice to stay in rapidly developing Southern California, ruralism with a small-town center would always remain his cherished ideal and the heart of his presentation of the good life to Americans. When a swimming pool was named in his honor in Marceline, Walt told the large crowd, "I'm glad my dad picked out a little town where he could have a farm, because those years that we spent here have been memorable years."

Disney is the biggest 20th-century promoter of Jeffersonian pastoralism covered in schmaltz. As Americans embraced the Industrial Revolution and flocked to cities in the aftermath of World War I, they were of two minds about it. Cities offered jobs, education, and advancement opportunities for the hard worker. They also were dirty, crowded, and full of the kind of temptations that the puritanical Elias Disney deplored even after economic failure forced him to leave his own farm behind for Kansas City. Disney mirrored the unease that many Americans felt about their growing urban areas. The Kansas City and Chicago of Walt Disney's Midwestern background were not the sunny Los Angeles where he would make his home base. Americans liked cities for their growth potential, but they also disliked them. To white Americans, cities represented a certain uneasy disturbing ambivalence. Places like New York City were rapidly filling with people from unfamiliar cultures, like Jews and Italians, who were perceived as not quite American by other Americans. Just as he wanted to spruce up Main Street and soothe out the most interesting corners, Walt also wanted to make the idea of the city into something less energetic, less messy, and more conformist. At the same time, he was always ready to use evolving technology and wanted it to be part of anything he did. Cities are places where ideas happen. Los Angeles is not tied to the past. Walt's Epcot was to be a more efficient, cleaner version of the American city. The city was a worldwide problem. Walt planned to solve it with American technology.

Epcot, along with Disney World, consumed much of Disney's energy during the last years of his life. When he bought 27,433 acres in central Florida in 1965, the land offered a lot of room for future expansion. For him, the question was what to fill it with. Disney World was to be only part of his plans for acreage more than three dozen times the size of Manhattan. His city, or Project X as it was originally called, would have a few basics that he thought made life better for residents, employers, and all visitors. The first was a central core. Dubbed "Progress City," the central city was supposed to have a commercial and business district where people could learn about new technologies in person. Next to it were to be several high-rise buildings where many of the residents would live as they worked in his city. He envisioned a 30-story convention center for travelers, with lots of annual events and a hotel to house them. A series of more low-rise housing options were to surround the central core, and there would be stores that carried goods from around the world. Residents and visitors alike were supposed to commute via monorail. Underneath it all, he saw roads for cars that people would take when leaving the city for other parts of the country.

The crowning glory of the place was to be a large glass dome that would shield residents from the worst effects of the Florida climate. Lots of covered subterranean roads were where all the dirty stuff would happen. Trucks would bring items in and take them out silently, efficiently, and quietly while residents went about their business. Disney's city was to be much like his other projects: a placid place without debris, managed by technology. In his concept, residents would choose to live there in part because they would have access to the latest technology. Companies could use the city's residents to test ideas before releasing them to the general public.

In the last frantic months before lung cancer took Walt's life, his employees were not sure what to make of his concepts. Many ideas, especially the dome covering the city, were clearly unworkable, while others, such as the monorail, were already being used in Disneyland. What Walt and his studio really needed was a partner. They wanted to find it in the Florida government. In a 25-minute film to the Florida legislature that can be seen on YouTube, Disney pleaded his case. The narration begins by talking about Disneyland. A voice intones, "An amusement park should offer more to the entire family. Here was no mere amusement park. Here was a whole new concept in entertainment where parents and children could have fun together." The film goes on to talk about Disney's other works, including his World Fair exhibits. Disney appears in person to demonstrate his plans for the entire site, including an airport, a high-speed, rapid-transit system, and Epcot. His pointer brings the audience to a large white blob, and then to more details that he calls a "community of tomorrow that will never be completed." This was to be "a showcase to the world for the ingenuity and imagination of American free enterprise."

Walt's "living blueprint of the future" was to take on a different character after his death. Florida lawmakers were entranced by the power of the Disney name. They gave Disney broad powers to do almost everything the company wished including (yes!) "the authority to generate power through nuclear fission." Working out the details of his vaguely fascist and utopian society took nearly two decades.

When Epcot finally opened to the public on October 1, 1982, the park was noteworthy in several ways. For one thing, as *Smithsonian Magazine* points out, it was "the single most expensive private construction project the world had ever seen." For another, it wasn't a city at all. Epcot was an amusement park. No Progress City or large residential area, let alone a dome to protect residents from the Florida climate, were to be seen. Epcot was not the Experimental Prototype Community of Tomorrow that Disney had in mind where people would live neat little lives, ever improved by technological progress. Instead, the park contained only a handful of his ideas, many of which were already in place in other parks. A monorail connected the park's sections. There was a permanent World's Fair in the form of 11 pavilions representing nations such as France and China. The Imagineers hosted spaces after the park opened known as Epcot Forums. Here, futurists like Ray Bradbury were encouraged to talk about what the future might hold and how to get there faster. The forum petered out once the Internet arrived in full force.

Epcot is not a place where the future is being developed. Today's Epcot is an example of what people thought the future might be like decades ago. Located in the same county as Disney World is a town called Celebration. Designed and built by Disney in the 1990s, Celebration is very much what Disney had in mind when he thought about the ideal place to live. There's lots of different types of houses with front porches, and plenty of appealing brick roads designed to invite pedestrian traffic. When Celebration was first brought to the public, the company had to hold a lottery because so many people wanted to live there. A decade later, Disney officials sold the town to a private equity firm for millions. Homes are more expensive here than in other parts of the area. A homeowner's association asserts tight control over the homes' details and look. Homeowners do not commute by monorail or live under a dome.

Epcot is one of the biggest of Disney's dreams, and arguably the least successful. Americans like the clean nostalgia that Disney represents, but they don't necessarily want to live under the company's control. The park also represents the company's innate limitations. While Disney changed America in many ways, its impact has many structural constraints. Walt Disney's very American city on a hill fell to the same forces that left Americans with the remnants of other utopian communities such as Bronson Alcott's Fruitlands and the Shakers. The real effect of his plans for Epcot were to allow the creation of Disney World and the lasting impact that the park has had on the development of Florida.

Growing Up Disney: Simple Animation with Complicated Themes

To be an American kid is to be immersed in the world of Disney at some point in life. Disney is everywhere. Just like kids had Mickey Mouse watches, Mickey Mouse lunch boxes, Mickey Mouse balls, and Mickey Mouse pillows in the 1930s, kids in the modern world have Disney movies on hand, the Disney Channel on television, and the Disney Store at their local mall. Commercials paint Disney World as the ideal family vacation spot. Children's books featuring Disney characters routinely climb the best-seller lists. Encountering Disney is *the* pervasive and universal experience of being a child in the United States. No matter what your socioeconomic status, location, sex, race, or other background, nearly all American children are united in having Disney in their lives. Disney has been a force for good in helping kids use their imagination. At the same time, the company's movies and other products have also forced an unwelcome homogenization onto what might otherwise be more diverse and enriching American childhood experiences.

Underneath what is an apparently placid surface, there's always been another side to Walt Disney and the Disney Studios that he left behind after he died. Animation has allowed the company to tell stories that might otherwise be more disturbing if they were shown as live-action films. That tug of war between the desire to tell a story and the desire to present a halcyon, serene view has long been part of the studio's work and part of its ultimate appeal. Even in the midst of movies for children, adults are introduced to complicated ideas and often compelling storylines.

Marketing to an audience of children was much of the focus of Disney's work as it began to develop over time. In his early days as a 19-year-old bringing Laugh-O-Grams to local Kansas City audiences, stories like "Little Red Riding Hood" formed the basis of his work rather than more adult options. *Steamboat Willie* features an adult, married mouse doing adult things, like avoiding work. Snow White lives with seven dwarfs who go off to their own jobs while she stays behind and plays mom and helpmeet. But most of his later work is all about children and their world. Disney always saw his main audience as kids and their parents. From the baby elephant in *Dumbo* to the children of *Peter Pan*, kids take center stage in his animated films. Kids are the point of his films and the point of view in almost every other work. The typical Disney hero is a teen on the cusp of adulthood. When adults are around, they're often depicted as incompetent hindrances, like the mom in *Mary Poppins,* or direct threats to the goodness of life, like the hunter who shoots Bambi's mother.

Disneyland and Disney World are all about families. Within the works that Disney presents to his audience, however, dark themes are a crucial part of the company's storytelling. They give it heft. Pinocchio is swallowed by a whale. The evil witch in *Snow White* tries to poison the title character. In *Lady and the Tramp*, the main character must deal with the arrival of a new baby, a theme that immediately resonated with children who have to cope with the arrival of a sibling. Scary, dark forests like the kind in fairy tales are an essential aspect of the Disney oeuvre. Disney was happy to explore them in the shows he presented to kids and adults. He did not shy away from tales that are meant to have depth to them.

Disney is largely thought of as a child's entertainment company because that is what it was for children. In series like *The Mickey Mouse Club,* the company never really got beyond the very simplest ideas. Nevertheless, there is a depth beneath the pastel surface. Works for mature audiences is a theme that the company has experimented with over time. For those at the studio, the question becomes how far they can push the company's wholesome image, and to what end. Despite what might seem to be a contemporary change of direction, a look at the work that Walt Disney and his animators did reveals that they were about more than just fairies or a simple pair of glass slippers. Disney movies have been pushing boundaries for a long time, and still often do.

The movie ratings by organizations such as the Motion Picture Association of America (MPAA) are a way of dividing movies into those that are suitable for children, those only for adults, and pornography. The definition of these terms has been a subject of long debate and a vital part of the history of the industry. Assigning a movie an overall holistic rating based on its content goes back as far as the beginning of movies. In Thomas Edison's *Carmencita*, produced in 1894, the main female character was often censored in part when shown to audiences because her on-screen dance revealed her underwear. Chicago became the first city to officially regulate movies in 1907. Separate pink permits were required to show films that city officials considered fit only for adult eyes. New York City mayor George B. McClellan closed hundreds of city theaters two years later because the city's police chief believed them to be unfit to view at all.

By 1915, the U.S. Supreme Court issued a decision agreeing with the formal right to censor films for the public in any way. Movies were viewed as a business rather than speech, and therefore not protected by the First Amendment. In response, the industry created its own standards. The Motion Picture Producers and Distributors of America allied themselves with the Catholic Church's Legion of Decency to create the Hayes Code. From 1930 until the mid-1950s, movies were required to meet the standards set forth by the Legion. Movies were formally rated by the organization. Those the church found objectionable in some way, such as the fact that a character was divorced, were given lower ratings. After a 1952 Supreme Court ruling that movies were indeed protected by the First Amendment, the industry began gradually changing its rating system.

In 1968, a new system was instituted by the MPAA. Movies were divided ranging from those wholly suited for children, with a G rating, to films given an X rating, meaning that no one under 17 was allowed to view them under any circumstances. Later additions would include a PG-13 rating, indicating that a movie has some material that might be considered inappropriate for elementary school–age children.

Walt Disney was happy to cooperate with the movie ratings system. It fit perfectly into his worldview. Not a single one of his movies were given anything other than the full approval of the Legion of Decency during his lifetime—despite the fact that many of them often dealt with adult ideas like coping with death and characters that engage in repeated acts of violence. Most of the films that the company produces today still have a G rating, even though they contain some content that might not be suitable for younger kids. Many works that have been produced in the aftermath of Walt's death, such as *Enchanted*, *Tangled*, and *Pocahontas*, continue to be aimed at children 10 and younger. Disney's animated features, with their use of vivid primary colors, easy-to-understand storylines, and accessible characters, are one of the foremost examples of American marketing and filmmaking intended for children. Animation often disguises actions in the company's films that would get more restrictive ratings if they were shown in live-action form. This is exactly what happened when the company introduced live-action versions of *The Lion King* (rated PG) and *Mulan* (rated PG-13).

In the 1970s, company officials began to take another look at the possible ways they could go with the direction of the studio's work. This led to the incorporation of some darker elements. *Mulan* is set during a war. In *The Hunchback of Notre Dame*, the villain kicks a young woman until she dies. *The Nightmare before Christmas* is a sophisticated romp where Santa Claus is kidnapped. Disney films in later years have also continued to grapple with extremely complicated themes, even as they occasionally fall short. *Pocahontas* is about colonialism, but has been criticized for its portrayal of the Native American experience. Nevertheless, a Disney animated film is almost automatically considered a virtuous effort by the film rating industry.

Animation has allowed the company to present material that has a certain intricacy and layering to it. This is part of a trend that is both historic and contemporary. When first introduced, many animated films and series such as *Felix the Cat* explored adult themes like alcoholism. Modern anime has a large adult audience, and adult themes to match. By bringing back characters who have jobs and work hard in animated features such as *Ratatouille* and *Zootopia*, the company is coming full circle back to the origins of the medium itself. As Disney Studios expands into new areas such as *National Geographic* and Marvel Entertainment, this is one trend that's likely to continue to make a mark on the studio and continue to challenge the image of Disney in the public's mind.

The Michael Eisner Era

By the time Walt Disney died, the company he left behind had finally found some measure of fiscal stability. No longer teetering on the edge of bankruptcy with each picture, many Disney Company officials felt that they could breathe more easily. Disneyland had thousands of visitors every single day and brought in enough revenue to finance all the company's other projects. Roy Disney took the company's Florida real estate holdings and turned the acreage into Disney World, an East Coast landmark. However, while the company undeniably had an impact on the way that the country saw itself, in the two decades after Walt's death, Walt Disney Studios was adrift. The public found the company's newer movies uninspired at best. What had been a devoted audience eager to lap up anything Disney might present was now largely indifferent at best towards many company efforts. Adults took their kids to Disney's movies and parks, but they did not expect much more than a few hours of amusement. The company was an established brand that seemed to lack energy and the willingness to step up and lead in innovative directions.

This would all change in the 1980s. One man would have an impact on the direction of the company in much the same way that Disney brothers had done before him. Michael Eisner spent 21 years at the helm of Disney. As chief executive officer (CEO), Eisner took the company to both new heights and new lows. His time at Disney mirrored the jubilant, arrogant American mood of the Reagan era and the perception of how America saw itself on the world stage. His leadership, like the leadership in the White House, was brash, self-confident, visionary, and expansive. Eisner's influence was also grandiose, occasionally thoughtless, and greedy to the point of absurdity. Eisner stepped into Walt's shoes and pushed the company into new areas of entertainment. He also brought in an orderly, more modern management style instead of the complacent, placid guidance of his predecessors. Eisner's vision would take the company beyond films and a few amusement parks and turn it into an indelible part of the American business landscape. When he was done, the company's stock, which once sold at about the price of a McDonald's cheeseburger, easily managed to meet the S&P 500 average and well beyond it. In a good year, the company was earning $100 million before he came along; by the time he left, earnings had risen into the billions. Fans still debate his ultimate legacy, but his impact is undeniable.

Michael Eisner came to Disney after being fired from Paramount Pictures. Unlike the working-class Disney brothers, Eisner came from money, attending private schools and making his home in a lavish New York City apartment. Yet like Disney, he was also relentlessly, ruthlessly ambitious. He made a series of bold moves that would expand the company's overseas ventures, bring movies from the Golden Age of Animation into people's lives again, push the world of marketing Disney characters even further than Kay Kamen had, widen the company's presence on television, and purchase some of the biggest names in American entertainment. Eisner's tenure mirrored the rise of Wall Street during the Reagan, Clinton, and George W. Bush years. His over-the-top pay and failure to share the wealth with his workers illustrates the impact of such policies on the lives of many American companies and their employees. His willingness to take risks also allowed the company to bring in new fans, again attracted to the magic of the Disney name.

Eisner made a few fundamental changes to the studio that expanded the company's reach in ways that Walt Disney had dreamed about but had not been able to bring to life. He took the company's library of movie classics and brought it to home viewers, opening up the company's vaults to earn profits and new fans. Eisner immediately spotted the possibility of the video cassette recorder (VCR) in the same way that Disney had spotted opportunity in television and other kinds of technologies. Where audiences previously had to go to movie theaters to see Disney films, they could now watch them at home, on their television sets. He demonstrated the power of the at-home movie market from the start. Families loved not having to go out to have a movie night. The re-release of movies on video made the company millions with little effort.

Like Disney, Eisner also tapped into the overseas markets with movies that had universal rather than specifically American themes. Under his direction, the company also pushed more adult-oriented movies that made it clear that the company was open to expanding beyond the G-rated market. Touchstone Pictures, a separate Disney division, churned out hits like *Pretty Woman, Splash,* and *Outrageous Fortune,* which earned huge profits and critical acclaim, but also attracted the ire of the religious right and put Disney's image as a provider of family entertainment at risk. Eisner shrugged off the criticism and plowed ahead anyway. The company also created several Disneylands in other parts of the world, continuing its overseas focus. These parks made the company a purveyor of the American experience internationally in ways that the movies had not quite managed. Opening entertainment venues in other countries put Disney in the role of ambassador. That was a role that Eisner sometimes bungled, but relished as a chance to put his own personal spin on the idea of the Disney park.

Eisner also established the company's role as the center of an entirely new media empire. ABC gave Walt Disney his start on television and the funds for the creation of Disneyland. Eisner bought the network in 1996 for a staggering $19 billion, along with other channels such as ESPN. He also revamped the company's animation division in a plan he called "the Disney Decade." Under his supervision, Disney became a going concern again. Massive animation hits like *Beauty and the Beast, Aladdin, The Lion King,* and *Pocahontas* once again made the name Disney synonymous with quality animation. His first 10 years at the helm of Disney saw triumph after triumph. Disney was back. Eisner arguably deserves the lion's share of the credit for it.

During the later years of his career at the company, Eisner's critics saw much to fault with the company's approach and his leadership. People pointed out to the company's infighting and what appeared to be petty arguments that drained Disney of its energy and focus. Insiders found Eisner's leadership lacking in many areas. Roy Disney, Walt's nephew, led a shareholder revolt against him. He accused Eisner of many mistakes, including being, "rapacious, soul-less, and always looking for the quick buck rather than long-term value which is leading to a loss of public trust." Roy Disney argued the theme parks Eisner had spearheaded, such as Disney's California Adventure, were done in a shoddy manner. In his view, the emphasis was on getting things done quickly and cheaply instead of meeting Disney's traditionally high standards. Other accusations made by top officials and major Disney shareholders included an invasive micromanagement strategy that brought down company morale and his failure to indicate who he thought should succeed him. Eisner spent much of his last two years in office countering these accusations rather than engaging in the kind of daring moves that had made his contributions so valuable in the first place.

When his tenure was all over, Eisner was a spent force. His departure ended not in death, but rather in a bare-bones goodbye that hardly made headlines at the company, let alone in the wider world. His 2005 final act was marked not with a giant celebration, but a whimpering email to company employees announcing he was taking his leave. Unlike Walt, he was no one's beloved uncle. Eisner would never become a well-known public figure, even as he cannily understood exactly what the public wanted from Disney.

While Eisner brought the company a second renaissance and some major blunders, the CEO furthered some other, less worthy goals. Like Disney's frenzied push for weekend work as the company produced *Snow White*, Eisner pushed workers hard. He had many top-level supporters who agreed with him. Studio chief Jeffrey Katzenberg smugly told the company's employees that "if you don't want to work Saturdays, don't bother coming in on Sunday." He was incredibly dismissive of workers asking for work-life balance and the fundamental company standards that previous Disney workers had fought so hard to attain. Decent working conditions and worker pay were not priorities for him or his fellow top executives. Company owners and top management like Walt Disney had seen themselves as a largely benevolent patriarchy where workers' needs were met in return for their loyalty. Management at the top of Disney after his death also saw their primary role as caretakers of the company's legacy rather than innovators during the 1970s.

The 1980s under Reagan would radically transform the notion of what it meant to be in charge of a company. CEOs were believed to shape their companies in the same way that a film director shaped a film. They thought that they should be compensated accordingly. Profits for shareholders were supposed to be their primary and ideally only goal. Eisner fit into the Coolidge capitalistic worldview that the business of America is business. He pushed the quest for profits to the top of the company's agenda.

Many of Eisner's ventures panned out, but others did not. An investment in the Internet search engine Infoseek foundered, even after he poured money into it. His colleagues at the top, even while feuding with him, were rewarded with profligate paychecks that raised eyebrows across the country. His protégé, Jeffrey Katzenberg, served with Eisner for a decade. He later sued for breach of contract and left with a settlement believed to be in the millions. Katzenberg would go to found DreamWorks, where he made his own mark with Academy Award–winning live-action films such as *American Beauty* and *Shrek*, the first picture to win the Academy Award for Best Animated Feature.

Eisner brought a whiff of crony capitalism when appointing friends to the company's board who were amply compensated. He also took hundreds of millions in compensation for himself, even during years when the company did not do well financially. Even as he took home gargantuan paychecks, the company came under fire for outsourcing the production of their toys to workers in Vietnam earning less than 10 cents an hour. Eisner's pay had parallels with the loss of worker clout during his time as CEO. Unlike Disney, he didn't suggest that workers were motivated by communism in asking for better working conditions and pay; however, he did say of theme park employees that trained monkeys could do their job just as well. In taking millions in salary, he represented an unwelcome trend sweeping the country. Outsized compensation packages like his were rapidly becoming the norm for a tiny handful of people, while ordinary workers saw either small raises or entirely stagnant pay. Many Disney workers had to turn to welfare to make ends meet. Work at the parks became just another dead-end job for many employees.

Eisner's successors would continue his policies of taking enormous paychecks. In 2019, Robert Iger was the entertainment field's highest-paid CEO, with annual compensation of over $40 million. This was down from a compensation package that had soared to over $65 million in 2016. Like Eisner before him, Iger has amassed a fortune of well over half a billion dollars while managing the company.

Eisner may have riled shareholders and made many missteps during his tenure. Disney's California Adventure lacks the kind of imagination and essential vision so valued in other parks. The park is a bare and not always inviting place that harks back to Coney Island instead of forging new directions in amusement parks. Yet the transformation of Disney from a movie studio and two theme parks into a company that redefined the world of American entertainment largely lies on his shoulders. His view of the company's place in the world must be seen on par with Walt Disney's. Eisner revived the company's animation division and oversaw films that can easily compete with the best of Walt Disney's work. His expansion into many other entertainment fields has enabled Disney to take a permanent seat at the table of American recreation. Thanks to him, Disney still has an outsized role to play in the world of American entertainment. Eisner cleared away the cobwebs and brought the company a new dynamism that bridged the gap between Walt Disney's death and the modern world.

An Eco-Friendly Theme Park: Animal Kingdom and the Environmental Movement

One of the most appealing aspects of the Disney Company is its ability to reinvent itself on a constant basis. Walt Disney rewarded workers who came up with new gags with bonuses. New ideas were always welcome, if not always brought to life as Disney envisioned. Company officials also continued to revisit old concepts that he began but did not finish during his tenure. One of his many plans incorporated his ideas about animals. Disney liked to say that his company started with a mouse. Animals were always on the agenda at Disney Studios, and Walt clearly loved them. Being around animals of all kinds reminded Walt of his brief years on a farm in the Midwest. As *Bambi* took shape, Disney brought in live fawns and deer so the animators could translate their movements to film. In movies like *Cinderella*, animals are there to help the main character realize her dreams.

Walt Disney was not the first person to show the world of nature through the lens of a camera, but he was the first person to create the idea of the nature documentary. Disney wanted pony rides at Disneyland and real jungle animals for his Jungle Cruise ride. After being told that that wasn't going to work, he came up with the idea of selling exotic animals at the park's stores. Luckily for moms squeamish about the idea of bringing home a python, the idea was shot down, but the notion of a Disney park with an animal theme remained.

In 1998, Disney revived the idea of an entire park designed for people and animals. Creatures of all kinds are the focus of Disney's Wild Animal Kingdom. Now known simply as Disney's Animal Kingdom, the park is similar to both zoos and other animal-themed amusement parks. First opened on Earth Day in 1998, the park was an instant hit with the public and continues to attract millions of people each year. Animal Kingdom combines a zoo, rides, and Disney-themed shows. The park can be divided into two parts. The first, overarching aspect of the park is a space devoted to the care and feeding of animals. More than 1,000 vets, zookeepers, and scientists are on the Disney payroll. They are entrusted with the care and feeding of over 2,000 animals living in the park. Workers watch over more than 300 animal species. Animal Kingdom has much in common with the more than 300 zoos that dot the American landscape. For many decades, zoos held animals in sparse iron cages that were little more than boxes. No thought was given to their care and presentation to the public beyond providing the animals with food, water, and some kind of shelter from the elements.

The movement to free animals of such confining spaces and think about how to present them to the public in a more humane manner began in the 1970s. Zoologists remade animal enclosures to more closely resemble the animals' actual habitats. They also sought to bring animals many of the same stimulants they might find in the wild. Instead of just giving them food, the goal was to make them work for it. Realistic toys and games were introduced to help the captive animals combat boredom. Zookeepers also sought to educate the public about the animals in front of them. Recreation and education were placed side by side. By the time Disney's Animal Kingdom opened, a fourth, overriding foundational concept was in place in the worldwide zoo movement—namely, conservation, the belief that the zoo should not merely show animals to the public but actively speak on their behalf. This movement has not been without controversy. Some advocates argue that conservation should mean freeing all animals and returning them to nature. Many others, such as those at Disney's Animal Kingdom, argue that a zoo can play a vital role in helping animals in the wild, while also allowing the public the chance to see and learn about many animals in person.

Animal Kingdom is the largest of the Disney parks by acreage. When it was in the process of being developed, animals in the park were brought in from other zoos. All the animals were required to be accredited by the Association of Zoos and Aquariums to ensure that the company was not working with poachers. Visitors can see familiar animals like lions and tigers in low-lying enclosures. They can also see endangered species such as cotton-top tamarins and western lowland gorillas. Zookeepers at the Animal Kingdom have been directly involved in efforts to keep up the number of certain animal species, such as the Guam kingfisher. More than three dozen kingfisher eggs have been hatched, which will help ensure the species avoids extinction. Disney officials have also promoted the park's mission in other ways. The Disney Conservation Fund, founded in 1995, has distributed over $100 million to conservation projects and organizations.

As part theme park and part activism, Animal Kingdom plays a unique role in the Disney universe. Walt Disney started out a staunch Democrat. In later years, he became a supporter of the Republican Party, but he largely kept his views out of the public eye. The public came to "The Happiest Place on Earth" to enjoy time in the sun, not hear political speeches. The Disney parks present a glossy view of American history where the pointy edges are sanded over. The Disney Company has largely kept out of politics. Company officials donate to both parties and make efforts to avoid being seen promoting any particular political issue. Animal Kingdom is really the only place in the company where visitors are almost ordered to change how they act in some way. Disney officials invite guests to do everything from visit the safari to see animals in the park's immense wildlife habitat to donate directly to conservation efforts.

Efforts of this kind tie in with other efforts that the company has been making to "go green." In 2018, the company announced that they would no longer provide visitors with single-use plastic straws and plastic stirrers. That same year, park officials also announced the creation of a 50-megawatt solar power facility. Located just outside Animal Kingdom, the solar facility provides enough power for two of the company's four Florida parks. It's part of an overall plan to reduce the company's net greenhouse emissions. Disneyland Paris relies in part on geothermal energy for fuel, while solar power is an integral part of Tokyo Disney's operations.

By putting out the message that they are trying to be part of the environmental movement, the company is once again acting in concert with the American public's viewpoint. Some critics have accused the company of using such efforts to put a gloss that ignores the true impact that it has on the Earth. When considering how far most visitors must travel to Disney parks, the company is hardly a corporate model for treading lightly on the Earth. The green movement is also an ironic turn for the company, given its history. Walt Disney was one of the nation's great promoters of the personal automobile. The Autopia ride awaited visitors when Disneyland first opened. The same ride would show up again in Disney World. Cars were shown to the public as the ultimate in personal liberation. Roy Disney knew that people would be happy to travel down the East Coast to visit his Florida park and escape the winter cold. When millions of people board a plane to visit the company's Disney's parks, they are adding tons of greenhouse gas to the environment. Given the company's vast impact on the national landscape, it is in a good position to push forward a discussion about abandoning reliance on fossil fuels and creating a greener America and a greener world.

On the Net: Legions of Adoring Fans and Disney+

When Italian poet Filippo Tommaso Marinetti first created the concept that would be known as futurism in 1908, he might have been writing part of the Disney manifesto. The Disney Company is very much focused on the past, or at least the past as seen through the eyes of Walt Disney. Within it lies a streak that is also focused on the future, or least the company's version of it. Walt Disney saw an ever-expanding way forward, in which things were constantly getting better for most people. Speed and youth formed the foundation of the Futurism movement. The movement was also based on the promise of technology.

These are the kinds of ideas that company officials have made their own. From the integration of sound with cartooning to the use of television and animatronics, technology has played a huge role in the company's foundation and plans. The use of technology has allowed the company to find new markets for their existing projects and develop brand-new projects at the same time. Today, the company continues to investigate new avenues. Like many companies, Disney has also found an outlet on the web.

The rise of the Internet has transformed how all the world's companies do business. From the American *Fortune* 500 company to stores selling items in Mongolia, the web is a vitally important sales outlet. Network television also makes up a huge part of the entertainment market in the United States. The larger networks continue to serve much of the American television market, with millions of viewers each night. Over time, larger networks have fragmented into clusters of smaller stations. Cable television opened up brand-new outlets for audiences and companies. Disney officials recognized this fact with the development of the Disney Channel. Started in 1983, the channel is a way of providing access to Disney-related materials in a single, convenient place.

The Disney Channel enjoyed enormous success when it was first unveiled. Today, Disney officials continue to use it as a vehicle for presenting varied types of programming to the public. More than 80 million Americans routinely tune in to watch original, first-run television series based on the Disney universe. They also enjoy access to theatrically released movies, as well as original movies designed specifically for the channel. In addition, the channel provides content for Disney Junior programs, aimed at children from 2 to 7 years old.

Disney Channel officials have come under fire for promoting what some critics perceive as less-than-ideal behavior. Some parent groups have accused the channel of promoting disrespectful behavior to teachers and other authority figures. They have also accused the company of promoting, as a *New York Post* editorial argued, "vulgar speech, crude jokes, and insolent behavior on a channel designed for kids." Such issues hark back to the original criticisms leveled at the company when it first released *Steamboat Willie*. Even as Disney has largely maintained a squeaky clean image, there has always been a spirit of subversion behind the company's work. The children in *Peter Pan* challenge adults. Kids are the heroes and focus in many Disney movies. Other critics argue that the network has done much to help kids learn new things. Blogger Zoey Norman points out, "*That's So Raven* shows kids that what makes them different also makes them powerful. *Good Luck Charlie* showed us that family, in all shapes, sizes, and forms, is where we find our strongest support systems. These shows shaped generations, and that is not something to scoff at. *Girl Meets World* discussed how people change as they grow up, teaches how to respect peoples boundaries," and makes the kids aware of the many important qualities they'll need as they grow up.

In recent years, segmentation in the American and global viewing markets have continued even further. Many Americans are no longer looking to television for most of their entertainment needs. Instead, they are turning to the Internet and highly specific individual network platforms. It's all about finding what people want and giving it to them exactly when they want it. Many viewers are looking for an on-demand option that lets them view series and movies when it is convenient for them, rather than on a network's or movie theater's predetermined schedule. Channels have arisen that focus on specific interests, such as sports, documentaries, or news. Once again, Disney has been there to meet viewers where they want to be right now.

The latest offering from Disney is Disney+. Like Netflix and Hulu, Disney+ is a streaming service based on the principle of on-demand viewing. Subscribers in dozens of countries from the United States to Singapore and Iceland pay a small fee each month. In turn, they have access to a vast library of materials in the Disney universe. Launched in late 2019, the service became an immediate hit, with over 50 million subscribers, within a short time. *Business Insider* describes the service as doing a "tremendous job anthologizing classic Disney movies and TV shows from decades ago that haven't been released in years and won't be available anywhere else." The focus of the service is access to the company's library of animated Disney classics. The library includes movies that have been left in the company's vault for years, as well as original programming, such as sequels to movies like *Frozen II* and *The Mandalorian*. The streaming service also includes access to properties that the company has acquired by purchasing such iconic programming as Marvel Comics, *The Simpsons,* and the *Star Wars* franchise. Viewers will find no R-rated material from any universe here, even though it is part of the Disney library of works.

Disney+ continues the company's tradition of showcasing family-centered options. Many parents have found it a highly useful part of their entertainment budget, as it allows them access to a huge library of children's movies and television shows for a relatively low price. The opening of the vault has also allowed viewers to get access to programming not seen in decades. In doing so, parents and Disney fans can see the evolution of the company over time. They can see everything from Disney's early shorts to the latest Pixar films. For animated film historians, Disney+ offers a treasure trove of material. Viewers can explore the progression of the company from one focused on the single idea of making animation match with music to a conglomerate that is virtually synonymous with American entertainment.

COVID-19, Disney, and the Future of the Amusement Park

Epidemics and pandemics are nothing new. Throughout history, humans have faced an unending succession of medical threats. Where this one was different was its truly global reach. By mid-2020, a brand-new and highly dangerous pandemic began. Known as COVID-19 or the coronavirus, the virus rapidly crossed borders in seemingly random patterns. A small handful of cases in China in 2019 laid the groundwork. The next 12 months would bring infection to hundreds of millions of people in nearly every single country. Leaders all over the world tried to figure out how best to cope with the impact of the virus on their communities. Much of the response focused on a few basic requirements that were intended to stop the spread of the infection. People were cautioned to follow social distancing guidelines and stay at least 6 feet away from each other. They were also asked to put on masks and wash their hands and other surfaces as often as possible. In addition, community leaders also asked people to stay home and avoid going out unless absolutely necessary.

While they were essential to stopping the spread of the disease, these measures had a huge impact on the global business community. Businesses all over the United States and the world were affected by the scope of the virus as it started to unfold. Certain industries were particularly hard hit. Tourism became nearly impossible except on a very local basis. As the virus traveled, community leaders across the globe shut down borders to travel between local places, as well as internationally.

In the United States, many state governors went so far as to tell people they must remain in their own states or within a certain geographical area such as New England or the mid-Atlantic states. Those who failed to obey these restrictions were fined and sent home when caught. Within a short time after the start of the pandemic, millions of Americans became infected. Millions more were facing all sorts of restrictions on their lives that were all about preventing even more cases. Business owners not deemed essential were told to shut down in many states. In big cities like Los Angeles and New York, the bodies piled up so high that staffers had to send corpses to the morgue in body bags, and loved ones were not allowed to organize funerals. Doctors and nurses were often forced to treat people in the street. Schools all over the country turned to remote learning to fill the gap, as parents were told to keep their kids home to avoid infecting teachers.

However, by the end of the year and into early 2021, researchers were able to develop highly effective vaccines that prevent COVID-19 in most people. Vaccinated people who become ill are far less likely to experience dangerous effects of the disease than their unvaccinated peers. American government and public officials offered access to the vaccines across the country based on a system that prioritizes the needs of people most at risk. That includes the elderly, as well as healthcare officials, teachers, and caregivers. The vaccine is available in the United States to anyone over the age of 12.

Like many other businesses, both Disneyland and Disney World were deemed nonessential and ordered to shut their doors to the public. Both parks had been briefly closed for a few times in the past for reasons ranging from hurricanes, the assassination of President John F. Kennedy, and the September 11 terrorist attacks. Walt Disney Studios also had faced massive reorganizations due to worker strikes and after World War II broke out. Nothing, however, could compare with the disruption caused by the complete shutdown of the parks due to the virus. Shutdowns for the parks began overseas with Shanghai Disneyland and Tokyo Disney. Other Disney venues, including Hong Kong Disneyland and Disneyland Paris, faced repeated openings and closings on an unpredictable basis depending on the rise and fall in the number of cases during certain time frames. This made it hard for fans in Asia and Europe to figure out when to make plans to visit. In China and Japan, the parks were open in 2020 only to local residents who could show they met the strict health requirements. For officials in Los Angeles and Florida, the choice was equally clear. As beloved as Disneyland and Disney World were in the public mind, both parks had to be shut in the interests of public safety. Officials in each state took different approaches, and so did officials at the company when it came to running each park. California state legislators ordered Disneyland to be closed completely for over a year. Floridian government officials ordered Disney World to close for a few months and then allowed the park to open again in the summer of 2020. Disney officials were given no choice in the matter, even after asking for exemptions from California state officials.

The two parks are quite different in nature, despite sharing much in common. As Dirk Libbey points out in an article for *Cinema Blend,* "Walt Disney World is actually part of the Reedy Creek Improvement District, a special municipal designation in Florida that gives Disney World control over its own destiny in many ways. So it almost is its own city, consisting not just of the four theme parks, but two water parks and over 20 hotels, all spread over two counties. By comparison, Disneyland Resort is two theme parks, three hotels and Downtown Disney, and you can walk from the theme park entrance plaza to the Disneyland Hotel at the far end of Downtown Disney in just a few minutes." Disneyland has no such stipulation. That difference has made managing the pandemic in California a lot harder, as Disney officials lack the same control over the park and the surrounding areas.

Officials at all of the American Disney parks have been criticized for not always adhering to social distancing and other health precautions. Executives were slow to close the American parks even though it was clear the pandemic was about to have a huge impact on Floridians and Californians. They also came under fire from consumer advocacy groups and elected officials for not doing more to protect workers and not adhering to social distancing requirements in the parks. Senator Elizabeth Warren of Massachusetts called out the company's layoff of over 25,000 workers while paying out shareholder dividends. However, she praised the company for picking up the tab for employees' healthcare during the layoffs. Numerous restrictions have been in place, although they are not always adhered to by workers and guests. Visitors to Disney World over 2 years old must wear masks. Everyone must submit to a temperature check. The park's fabled "character meet-and-greets" have been replaced by socially distanced character procession that are likely to continue as the epidemic continues.

In an effort to offset the restrictions and make people happier, guests attending Disney World were given deep discounts. Disney World suspended features like the Fastpass, closed many restaurants, and installed plexiglass dividers. Despite these efforts, many visitors felt that the company did not do enough to protect their safety. Critics chided the park for being very crowded in the middle of a pandemic and telling the world that it was safe to attend. They also criticized the company for allowing longer lines while closing certain attractions. Others praised it for using technology to ensure social distancing via mobile ordering at restaurants and giving cast members effective instructions about wearing masks and enforcing Florida state hygiene regulations. The Actors' Equity Association, which represents Disney World performers, called for the park's complete closure in the name of safety.

For Disney executives, the pandemic has been one of the greatest obstacles the company has ever faced. Billions of dollars in losses followed during the quarter following the rise of the virus, even as they rebounded once Disney World opened again and people signed up in greater numbers for Disney+. When the parks are not operating, the company faces massive revenue loss. The parks are likely to experience a resurgence in popularity and revenues as their doors reopen to full capacity once most people are vaccinated. However, it is not clear what policies might be in place should there be a new, vaccine-resistant mutation or a new pandemic. In an effort to manage the reopening of Disneyland and see how crowds will respond, park officials offered access to Disney California Adventure. No rides were operating, but people could walk around the park and buy food and merchandise. The $75 price includes both parking fees and a $25 food voucher. Offered to the public on March 4, tickets were sold out in less than a day.

Clearly, despite its recent difficulties, Disney is not the company or the place it was when Walt Disney first came to California. What was once a single idea is now a huge company with a large library of works and a ready audience for its products all over the world. The modern Walt Disney Company has deep pockets and tremendous resources. The entertainment company and the parks they service will endure even in the middle of a global pandemic. From a tiny idea about an animated mouse, Walt Disney crafted an organization that truly defines what it means to be an American and what an all-American company is.

Bibliography

Barrett, Stephen M. *Hidden Mickeys: A Field Guide to Walt Disney World's Best Kept Secrets*. 8th ed. SMB Books, 2017.

Bendazzi, Giannalberto. *Cartoons: One Hundred Years of Cinema Animation*. Indiana University Press, 1995.

Bernardi, Daniel, Murray Pomerance, and Hava Tirosh-Samuelson. *Hollywood's Chosen People: The Jewish Experience in American Cinema*. Wayne State University Press, 2013.

Biskind, Peter. *Easy Riders, Raging Bulls: How the Sex-Drugs-and-Rock 'n' Roll Generation Saved Hollywood*. Simon & Schuster, 1999.

Brode, Douglas. *Multiculturalism and the Mouse: Race and Sex in Disney Entertainment*. University of Texas Press, 2006.

Canemaker, John. *Winsor McCay: His Life and Art*. Artabras, 1990.

Crafton, Donald. *Before Mickey: The Animated Film, 1898–1928*. University of Chicago Press, 1995.

Dakin, Glenn. *Disney Villains: The Essential Guide*. DK Children, 2020.

Darcy, Jen. *Disney Villains: Delightfully Evil: The Creation The Inspiration The Fascination*. Disney Editions, 2016.

Davis, Amy M. *Good Girls and Wicked Witches: Women in Disney's Feature Animation*. John Libbey Publishing, 2007.

Emerson, Chad Denver. *Project Future: The Inside Story behind the Creation of Disney World*. Ayefour Publishing, 2010.

Fanning, Jim. *The Disney Book: A Celebration of the World of Disney*. DK, 2015.

Finch, Christopher. *The Art of Walt Disney: From Mickey Mouse to the Magic Kingdoms*. Portland House, 1988.

Fogelsong, Richard. *Married to the Mouse: Walt Disney World and Orlando*. Yale University Press, 2003.

Gabler, Neal. *An Empire of Their Own: How the Jews Invented Hollywood*. Penguin Random House, 1988.

Gabler, Neal. *Walt Disney: The Triumph of American Animation*. Alfred A. Knopf, 2006.

Gennawey, Sam. *Walt and the Promise of Progress City*. Theme Park Press, 2014.

Gerstein, David. *Walt Disney's Mickey Mouse. The Ultimate History*. TASCHEN, 2018.

Goldberg, Aaron. *Buying Disney's World: The Story of How Florida Swampland Became Walt Disney World*. Quaker Scribe, 2021.

Goldberg, Aaron. *The Disney Story: Chronicling the Man, the Mouse, and the Parks*. Quaker Scribe, 2016.

Hack, Richard. *The Rise and Fall of Michael Eisner: The Man behind the Mouse*. New Millenium, 2004.

Hold, Nathalia. *The Queens of Animation: The Untold Story of the Women Who Transformed the World of Disney and Made Cinematic History*. Little, Brown and Company, 2019.

Iger, Robert. *The Ride of a Lifetime: Lessons Learned from 15 Years as CEO of the Walt Disney Company*. Random House, 2019.

The Imagineers. *Walt Disney Imagineering: A Behind the Dreams Look at Making MORE Magic Real*. Disney Editions, 2010.

Johnson, Mindy. *Ink & Paint: The Women of Walt Disney's Animation*. Disney Editions, 2017.

Johnston, Ollie. *The Illusion of Life: Disney Animation*. Disney Editions, 1995.

Kinni, Theodore. *Be Our Guest: Perfecting the Art of Customer Service*. Disney Editions, 2011.

Korkis, Jim. *EXTRA Secret Stories of Walt Disney World: Extra Things You Never Knew You Never Knew*. Theme Park Press, 2018.

Korkis, Jim. *Who's Afraid of the Song of the South? And Other Forbidden Disney Stories*. Theme Park Press, 2012.

Kothenschulte, Daniel. *The Walt Disney Film Archives. The Animated Movies 1921–1968*. TASCHEN, 2020.

Kurtti, Jeff. *The Art of Disney Costuming: Heroes, Villains, and Spaces Between*. Disney Editions, 2019.

Kurtti, Jeff. *Travels with Walt Disney: A Photographic Voyage around the World*. Disney Editions, 2018.

Lutz, E. G. *Animated Cartoons: How They Are Made, Their Origin and Development*. Charles Scribner's Sons, 1920.

Masters, Kim. *Keys to the Kingdom: How Michael Eisner Lost His Grip*. William Morrow, 2000.

Merritt, Russell, and J. B. Kaufman. *Walt in Wonderland: The Silent Films of Walt Disney*. Johns Hopkins Press, 2000.

Murguía, Salvador Jimenez (ed.). *The Encyclopedia of Racism in American Films*. Rowman & Littlefield, 2018.

Nichols, Chris. *Walt Disney's Disneyland*. TASCHEN, 2018.

Pierce, Todd James. *The Life and Times of Ward Kimball: Maverick of Disney Animation*. University Press of Mississippi, 2019.

Sito, Tom. *Drawing the Line: The Untold Story of the Animation Unions from Bosko to Bart Simpson*. University Press of Kentucky, 2006.

Smothers, Marcy Carriker. *Eat Like Walt: The Wonderful World of Disney Food*. Disney Editions, 2017.

Snow, Richard. *Disney's Land: Walt Disney and the Invention of the Amusement Park That Changed the World*. Scribner, 2019.

Spiegel, Joshua. *Walt's Original Sins: Disney and Racism*. Theme Park Press, 2018.

Stewart, James B. *DisneyWar*. Simon & Schuster, 2006.

Sweet, Matthew. *Inventing the Victorians: What We Think We Know about Them and Why We're Wrong*. St. Martin's Press, 2001.

Taylor, John. *Storming The Magic Kingdom: Wall Street, the Raiders, and the Battle for Disney*. Knopf, 1987.

Thomas, Robert. *Walt Disney: An American Original*. Disney Editions, 1994.

Index

Academy Awards, 8, 10, 15, 36, 41, 125
Aladdin, 86, 92, 123
Alaska, 15
Alice in Wonderland, 16, 19, 36, 53, 79, 84, 96
Anaheim, CA, 47, 51, 58, 61, 62, 64, 66, 67

Bambi, xiv, 11, 16, 19, 20, 35, 91, 95, 97, 114, 119, 126
Barré, Raoul, 27
Beauty and the Beast, 86, 92, 93, 123
Blackton, James Stuart, 27
Bluth, Don, 39
Brave, 93
Bray, John Randolph, 28

California, 5, 20, 48, 51, 55, 60, 61, 62, 63, 65, 68, 69, 74, 80, 84, 111, 112, 115, 134
Canada, 2, 55
Carroll, Lewis, 16
Celebration, Florida, xiii, 117–118
Chaplin, Charlie, 29, 35
Chicago, Illinois, xii, 2, 21, 24, 46, 49, 62, 115, 120
Chicago Academy of Fine Arts, 4
China, 25, 67, 68, 117, 131, 132

Cinderella, 7, 16, 39, 79, 86, 91, 93, 96, 97, 111, 114, 126
Cold War, 1
Coney Island, 46–47, 49, 53, 61, 66, 125
COVID-19, 131–134
Cuba, 14

Davy Crockett television series, 18, 53, 80–81, 82, 83
de Seversky, Alexander, 13
Der Führer's Face, 13
Disney, Elias, 2, 3, 50, 63, 66, 115
Disney, Flora, 2
Disney, Herbert, 65
Disney, Lillian, 22, 30, 55
Disney, Roy, 5, 9, 16, 19, 22, 23, 24, 37, 38, 41, 42, 55, 62–67, 73, 74, 77, 85, 89, 108, 121, 128
Disney, Ruth, 2
Disney, Walt
  ABC, 17–18, 19, 20, 43, 53, 54, 56, 80, 83, 123
  Academy Award for Best Animated Short Film, 8
  anti-Semitism charges, 98–100
  birth, xii, 2
  childhood, xiii
  daughters, 22, 42, 49, 90
  death, xi, 20, 44, 63, 85

Disney Bros., 5, 6, 14
Disney Channel, 42
father (*see* Disney, Elias)
Golden Age of Animation, 14, 31, 35, 38, 41, 47, 122
Iwerks-Disney Commercial Artists, 5
Mickey and the Beanstalk, 14
paper route, 3
racism charges, 101–106
Retlaw Enterprises, 42
South America, 12
television, 14, 16, 80
True-Life Adventure series, 15
Uncle Walt, xii, 2, 17, 21, 33, 65, 107
Walt Disney Presents, 17, 18
Disney Channel, 42, 82, 92, 105, 118, 129–130
Disney Studios, 8, 13, 15, 20, 25, 35, 40, 45, 95, 96, 105, 110, 118, 121
Disney World, 22, 24, 106
Disneyland, xiv, 17, 19, 20, 23, 46, 50–60, 62, 65, 68, 80, 84, 106, 111, 123, 126, 132
Disneyland Paris, 68–69, 70, 89, 111, 128, 132
Disney+, 23, 105, 130–131
Disney's Animal Kingdom, 23, 67, 115, 126–128
Disney's California Adventure, 59, 124–125, 134
Disney's Hollywood Studios, 23, 54
Donald Duck, 12, 45, 78
Dumbo, 9, 10, 35, 51, 79, 86, 91, 103, 119

Ebert, Roger, 86, 102
Edison, Thomas, 26, 120
Eisenhower, Dwight D., 18, 55
Eisner, Michael, 42, 43, 87, 108, 121–126

Epcot, 23, 47, 60, 62, 64, 67, 90, 114–118

Fantasia, xiv, 9, 10–11, 32, 35, 86, 90, 95, 103, 107, 109
Felix the Cat, 27, 29, 30, 31, 121
Fleischer, Max, 28
Florida, 2, 20, 24, 61, 62, 63, 64, 66, 68, 69, 84, 89, 90, 111, 117, 121, 133
France, 7, 26, 68, 90, 117
Freleng, Friz, 29
Frozen, 93, 97

Gabler, Neal, 32, 75, 77, 98
George Borgfeldt & Company, 73–75, 76
Gertie the Dinosaur, 27, 28
Great Depression, 8, 13, 21, 33, 47, 76, 108
Griffith, D. W., 49, 102

Hearst, William Randolph, 28
Hitler, Adolf, 12
Hollywood, xii, 5, 6, 23, 48, 49, 54, 58, 75, 85, 94, 98, 99, 100, 101, 103, 113
Holt, Nathalia, 95, 96, 97, 104, 106
Hong Kong Disneyland, 69–70, 132
Hurd, Earl, 28

Iger, Robert, 30, 41, 43, 105
IMAX, 15
Ising, Rudolf, 29
It's a Small World After All, xiv, 90, 97
Iwerks, Ub, 5, 30, 31

The Jazz Singer, 6
Jolson, Al, 6

Kamen, Herman "Kay," 73–79, 80, 101, 122
Kansas City, MO, 2, 3, 5, 21, 47, 49, 50, 74, 115, 119

Index

Kansas City Film Ad Company, 5, 29
The Karnival Kid, 7
Knott's Berry Farm, 50

Lady and the Tramp, 16, 36, 103, 119
Laugh-O-Gram Studio, 5, 29, 119
The Lion King, 24, 39, 91, 121
The Little Mermaid, 39
Little Nemo, 28
Los Angeles, 5, 6, 16, 21, 47, 48, 49, 50, 61, 66, 75, 115, 132, 133
Lumière brothers, 26

Magic Kingdom, 67
Main Street, U.S.A., xiii, 20, 51, 54, 65
Marceline, MO, 2, 3, 21, 115
March of the Penguins, 15
McCay, Winsor, 28
Messmer, Otto, 28, 29
MGM Studios, 36
Mickey Mouse, xiv, 5, 7, 8, 17, 27, 29, 30, 31, 32, 35, 36, 45, 59, 67, 70, 71, 73, 74, 76, 77, 78, 79, 83–84, 85, 91, 118
Mickey Mouse Club, xiii, 81–83, 119
Miller, Ron, 38, 42, 85
Minnie Mouse, xiv, 6, 31, 67, 70, 72, 76, 91
Mintz, Charles, 6, 30
Missouri, xiii, 51
Mulan, 24, 39, 71, 91, 121

NBC, 16
New York City, 5, 29, 61, 73, 74, 76, 80, 98, 116, 120, 122
New York Times, 12, 43, 77, 78, 81, 105
Nolan, Bill, 28

One Hundred and One Dalmatians, 37, 38, 97

Orlando, Florida, 23, 24, 38, 61, 62, 65, 66, 70

Pearl Harbor, 10, 12
Peter Pan, 16, 79, 96, 97, 102, 119, 130
Pinocchio, 9, 10, 35, 86, 87, 105, 109, 111, 119
Pixar, xiv, 40–41, 43, 93, 131
Pocahontas, 39, 93, 120, 121, 123
Pribilof Islands, 15
Prince Charming, 9
The Princess and the Frog, 106

Reagan, Ronald, 58, 82
Red Cross Ambulance Corps, 4
Reynaud, Émile, 26
RKO, 7, 15
Roosevelt, Franklin Delano, 12, 13, 38, 109
Rotoscoping, 28

Saludos Amigos, 12
Shanghai Disneyland, 70, 132
Silly Symphonies, 8, 33
Sleeping Beauty, 36, 39, 45, 87, 92, 96
Snow White and the Seven Dwarfs, 8–9, 10, 13, 14, 19, 22, 23, 29, 32–36, 38, 39, 40, 41, 51, 52, 67, 76, 77, 78, 87, 91, 95, 100, 109, 111, 113, 119, 124
Song of the South, 14, 15, 101, 103, 105–6, 114, 136
St. Louis, 2, 61
Star Wars, 53, 71, 72, 85, 131
Steamboat Willie, 6, 7, 18, 29, 30, 31, 32, 35, 67, 72, 73, 74, 99, 108, 113, 119, 130
Steeplechase Park, 46
Stokowski, Leopold, 10

Technicolor, 32
Terry, Paul, 28

The Three Caballeros, 12
Tivoli Gardens, 46
Tokyo Disney, 68, 106, 128, 132
Touchstone Pictures, 23, 42, 123
Toy Story, 41, 114
Treasure Island, 16

United Artists, 7
Universal Studios, 88

Victory through Air Power, 13

Walt Disney World, 19, 63–67, 68, 85, 88, 116, 118, 132, 133, 134
Warner Bros., 30, 35, 36, 106, 110
Winkler, Margaret, 6
World War I, 4, 115
World War II, 7, 11, 13, 21, 24, 67, 95, 132

About the Author

Stacy Mintzer Herlihy is a freelance writer based in New Jersey. She lives with her husband, daughters, and two very spoiled mush cats. She is the coauthor of *Your Baby's Best Shot: Why Vaccines Are Safe and Save Lives*. She is also the author of *Smoking: Your Questions Answered*. In addition, her writing has appeared in many publications.

www.ingramcontent.com/pod-product-compliance
Lightning Source LLC
Chambersburg PA
CBHW060956230426
43665CB00015B/2224